Henry George Hunt

A concise history of music from the commencement of the Christian

era to the present time

For the use of students

Henry George Hunt

A concise history of music from the commencement of the Christian era to the present time
For the use of students

ISBN/EAN: 9783337259624

Printed in Europe, USA, Canada, Australia, Japan

Cover: Foto ©Thomas Meinert / pixelio.de

More available books at **www.hansebooks.com**

A CONCISE

HISTORY OF MUSIC

FROM THE COMMENCEMENT OF THE CHRISTIAN ERA

TO THE PRESENT TIME.

For the Use of Students.

BY

H. G. BONAVIA HUNT, B.Mus.,

CHRIST CHURCH, OXFORD,

WARDEN OF TRINITY COLLEGE, LONDON;
AND LECTURER ON MUSICAL HISTORY IN THE SAME COLLEGE.

New Edition, Revised.

NEW YORK:

CHARLES SCRIBNER'S SONS,
SUCCESSORS TO
SCRIBNER, ARMSTRONG & CO.

TO

MY DEAR AND HONOURED FRIEND,

SIR JOHN GOSS, MUS. D.,

WITHOUT WHOSE NAME

NO HISTORY OF MODERN MUSIC CAN BE COMPLETE,

This little Book

IS,

WITH EVERY FEELING OF RESPECT AND AFFECTION,

INSCRIBED.

December, 1877.

PREFACE TO THE SECOND EDITION.

THAT a new edition of this little work should be called for within three months of its first appearance affords gratifying evidence that it has met—to some extent, at least—an acknowledged want among students of music.

In response to the general invitation with which I concluded my "Introductory" Chapter, several correspondents have favoured me with corrections and suggestions of which I have thankfully availed myself. Accordingly, a few minor names and matters have been added or substituted for others. The general plan and the bulk of the work, however, remain the same as before.

I cannot let this occasion pass without expressing my sincere obligations to those gentlemen, the majority of them musicians of acknowledged learning and eminence in the art, who have assisted me in the careful preparation of this Second Edition for the press.

H. G. B. H.

March, 1878.

CONTENTS.

———◇———

INTRODUCTORY.

THE plan of this little History is so distinct—as far as I am aware—from that of any other work upon the same subject, that a careful perusal of these prefatory explanations will greatly help the reader in his study of the book. It would be more correct to say that all previous Histories of Music are distinguished from the present effort in the respect that they have no plan at all, beyond the two very general features of chronological order (rarely adhered to) and a grouping of composers and events into a number of "schools." The voluminous works of Burney and Hawkins each form a mass of promiscuous and ill-digested matter, which requires much sifting and collating on the part of the student before he can arrive at the information he requires; while, as both works are now a century old, they stop short of the most productive as well as the most interesting period of musical history. The smaller histories of Hogarth, Schlüter, Ritter, and others, though admirably adapted for the purpose for which they were originally compiled, are still no more than courses of popular lectures, in which much that is naturally required for a student at a musical examination, is necessarily omitted.

The classification adopted in the following pages is the result of many trying experiences as a student, whose chief difficulty has been the separation of the subjective from the objective divisions of the study. To a certain extent the one is necessarily wedded to the other, and I have recognized this where necessary,—yet without disturbing the general plan, which I will now proceed to describe.

The book is divided into Three Sections.

The First Section contains a general review of musical epochs and events, including short biographical sketches of the principal characters concerned, with an enumeration of their most important works. The principle of chronological order has been observed, yet not slavishly, as sometimes it would have seriously interfered with the general plan, without yielding an equivalent advantage. A palpable difficulty has been the classification of the " schools." The term " school " is so ambiguous, and has been employed in so many senses, that the student is frequently at a loss when asked to define any one of them. There are the " Belgian " or " Flemish," the " Roman," the " Venetian," the " Neapolitan," the " Spanish," the " German," the " French," the " English " schools ; and these terms have respectively been variously and indiscriminately used to denote either a group of composers of the same nationality, or a distinguishing style of musical composition. Again, as to the latter interpretation of the term, the student, in the course of his reading, is liable to a new bewilderment with every succeeding work he is led to peruse. Some writers adopt the above classification; others speak broadly of two great contrasting schools—the Italian and the German; others, again, add to these two the French and the English schools; while a fourth section will deny or ignore the existence of the English school *in toto.* In order to disencumber the mind of such perplexities as these, I have generally adopted the method of classification by nationality; and have included the Roman, Venetian, and Neapolitan groups under the common head of "Italian." On an examination of the text of the first section, the reader will notice that beyond paragraph 18, every paragraph, with a few exceptions, is headed with an initial letter enclosed in brackets. Each initial letter denotes the division to which the matter that follows it belongs; viz., **B.**, Belgian; **I.**, Italian; **G.**, German; **E.**, English; **F.**, French. These paragraphs are so worded that the reader, according to his requirements, may trace the course of any particular "school" without interruption. Thus, if at any time he wish to confine his attention to the succession of English composers, he will look for the first paragraph headed by the initial **E.**, after which his eye will easily and rapidly guide him to the second and further paragraphs bearing the same initial letter. And as far as the succeeding paragraphs of each denomination are concerned, the chronological order will be found intact.

The Second Section comprises a series of Chronometrical Tables or Charts, the first Chart containing 1000 years, the succeeding Charts 100 years. Each

Chart is duplicated, and the duplicates are placed on opposite pages. The right hand duplicate contains the names of musicians and historians, while that on the left hand is devoted to the corresponding epochs and events. As in a geographical map the relative positions of towns or counties may be seen at a glance, so in this Chronological map the student may see pictured before him, upon a very simple plan, the time-relationship of persons and events,—persons with persons, events with events, and events with persons. For this admirable scheme I am indebted to my able and learned friend, Mr. David Nasmith, LL.B., whose Chronometrical Chart of English History has formed the model for these tables. The study of History, with its legion of miscellaneous facts and disjunct dates, has by this invention been rendered far less irksome and more definite, and it is a matter for regret that Mr. Nasmith's valuable Chart is not to be found on the walls of every school-room in England, notwithstanding the earnest recommendations of Brougham, Thiers, Carlyle, and other eminent historians.

The Third Section summarizes the history of the art itself, unencumbered by the necessity of tracing the career of any composer referred to in the course of the text. It deals (1) with the birth and development of the modern scales, counterpoint and harmony ; (2) with the history of choral music, ecclesiastical and secular; (3) with instrumental music, and the development of the now classical forms of composition ; (4) with musical instruments, ancient and modern ; and enumerates (5) some of the principal works of each important class, together with the names of composers, arranged in approximate chronological order.

The student is warned that he is not to expect in this what is called a "readable" book; it has been written with a view to systematic study, and not for mere entertainment,— in short, it is a text-book, not a discourse. To this end I have endeavoured throughout to restrict myself to matters of fact, every digression being an attempt to throw light upon facts disputed or uncertain. These pages, then, are not intended for consecutive perusal, but for sectional study; each division, while maintaining a relation with the whole, being complete as to its own subject. I would therefore recommend, first, a cursory perusal of the work from beginning to end, in order to master the plan and gain a general idea of the contents; secondly, to select any school or period treated of in the General Summary; thirdly, to refer, as occasion may require, to the corresponding text of the Art Summary; and lastly, to consult the Chronometrical Tables for the period in question—or, better still, to copy out such Tables upon a separate sheet, and upon a larger scale, that they may lie immediately in front of the student while he is reading. Each of the sections may be studied as a principal text, and compared with the other sections in the same way. For example, if the student take for his subject the growth and development of the Sonata form, he will read Section III., paragraphs 26—28 ; if he wish for particulars respecting the principal composers mentioned in par. 28, he will refer to Section I.; who were contemporary writers of Sonatas he will ascertain at a glance from the Tables in Section II. ; and so on, *mutatis mutandis*, according to the nature of the subject in hand. The student is thus enabled to take a more or less comprehensive view of any subject in proportion to his individual requirements. The miscellaneous questions at the end of the book have been added as an assistance to students preparing for examinations.

Having, by a systematic study of these pages, possessed himself of the principal facts of Musical History, the student will be the better able to understand and appreciate the more critical writings of other historians, and to every advanced student such reading is recommended as an after course.

Lastly, in a work containing an enormous number of facts and dates, some of them controverted or otherwise uncertain, it is to be feared that occasional discrepancies, real or apparent, may be found. I shall be grateful to any reader who will communicate to me any such errors or discrepancies, with a view to correction upon the first opportunity. As to omissions, the necessary limits of the work have precluded the insertion of many names and particulars of secondary importance, but I hope and believe that the information supplied is amply sufficient for the needs of the ordinary student of music.

Trinity College,
London, W.

HISTORY OF MUSIC.

SECTION I.

GENERAL SUMMMARY.

1. WHILE in the works of many of the ancient writers the subject of Music has been dwelt upon at more or less length, it is impossible for us to form upon their statements or passing allusions an exact idea of the character or extent of the art as practised in the days of the Egyptian, Grecian, and Roman empires.*

2. With regard to the musical scales of the Greeks, all that we really know is :—That they were built on a system of *tetrachords*—or groups of four notes ascending in diatonic succession ; that, familiarly speaking, two of these tetrachords put together formed a " scale ; " that there were various kinds of scales, differing in nature from each other in respect of the relative positions occupied by the semitones ; and that, therefore, the effect of the music, whether melody or harmony, produced from such scales, was entirely different from that of the present day.

3. It is generally believed that the Greeks originally derived the rudiments of their musical knowledge from the Egyptians, who were great proficients in the art, as

---

* " In short, there can be no history of music as an art, where no musical works of art exist."—SCHLÜTER.

1

may be seen from the monumental remains of that
splendid nation.   Upon a number of these monuments
are representations of harps, lutes (or guitars), and
other instruments ; bands of musicians performing concerted music ; but in the nature of things there is no
source from which we may gain any notion as to the
effect or character of the music produced.

4. There has been much discussion on the question
whether harmony was known to, or employed by, the
ancients.   On the one side it is asserted that the Greek
writers make no mention of harmony * (as we understand the term) in any of their works upon music, and
that the construction of the old scales—the discordant
nature of their " thirds," for instance—effectually precluded the use of polyphonic music.   On the other side,
the existence of the stringed instruments, such as the
lyre, the harp, and the lute ; the structure of the double
pipes blown by a single mouthpiece ; have been adduced
as strong evidence in favour of some sort of harmony,
however crude it might sound to modern ears.

5. The most noted among Greek theorists were
Pythagoras (*circ.* B.C. 600) and **Lasos**; amongst
practical musicians were **Terpander** of Lesbos (B.C.
670), who invented or introduced the seven-stringed
kithara; **Olympos** the Phrygian, who brought into
Greece the art of flute-playing, which thenceforward
formed an important element in Greek instrumental
art; and **Tyrtæus**, a soldier, musician, and poet,—who
in fact was a " troubadour," or minstrel.

6. Although it is tolerably conclusive that instrumental music, pure and simple, was a favourite recre-
ation of the Egyptians, the Greeks for many ages
employed their instruments only as an accompaniment
to the voice, whether for monologue or chorus.   It is

---

* The term ἁρμονία (harmonia), as employed by Greek writers,
is applied only to their octave system, or conjunction of two
successive tetrachords (*v.* par. 10).

characteristic of the race that the later development of flute-playing as a separate art was accompanied by the institution of competitive trials of skill, by which the real vocation of the musician was lost amid the petty technicalities of mere mechanical display. And upon this began the decline of Grecian music, which indeed practically died out with the fall of the Grecian empire.

7. The Romans had no distinctive music of their own. They were pre-eminently a martial race, and probably the music they most appreciated was the trumpet-call. In their earlier days they were too busy, and in later times too lazy, to cultivate the art among themselves. In the era of luxury and dilettanteism which preceded their decay, they employed Greek slaves as singers and players. In the reign of Nero, who affected a devotion to music, the pursuit of the art became fashionable for a time, but the Romans were not in earnest, and consequently left behind them no marks of musical culture.

8. It is not until the fourth century after Christ that the actual history of music as a separate art begins. About the year A.D. 330, Pope **Sylvester**, we are informed, instituted a singing school in Rome, but there is no statement upon which we may form an accurate idea of the kind of music practised. By the light, however, of subsequent events we know that the singing must have been unisonal, and that the melodies were built upon the old Greek scales or modes, or possibly were ancient Hebrew airs, though some good authorities consider this doubtful. We also infer that St. Sylvester was acquainted with the method of antiphonal chanting, as Pliny, who lived in the second century, incidentally mentions this as the custom amongst the Christians of his day.

9. A few years later (374—397) **St. Ambrose**, Archbishop of Milan (not the Ambrose to whom is attributed the authorship of the *Te Deum*), took an especial interest in the culture of Church music, and arranged

the four diatonic scales known as "The Authentic Modes." He decreed that upon one or other of these scales all Church melodies should be constructed, and during his time many new hymns or chants were composed, some of them by himself. St. Ambrose also greatly improved the style of antiphonal singing, and organized a fine choir in his own church at Milan.

10. St. Ambrose had no immediate successor to continue the excellent work he had begun. By degrees the music of the Church deteriorated ; and it was not until two centuries had elapsed that a reform was effected. **Gregory** the Great (590—604) during his pontificate devoted himself to the work of reformation and improvement, and restored to Church song that solemnity of character which it had gradually lost. He also added to the Ambrosian scales four others, which he called " the *plagal* modes." Both the authentic and plagal modes have for their foundation the old Greek system of " tetrachords." We annex a complete table of the eight scales :—

Tone	Authentic.	Tone	Plagal.
1. Dorian.	D E F G A B C D	2. Hypo-Dorian (or Æolian).	A B C D E F G A
3. Phrygian.	E F G A B C D E	4. Hypo-Phrygian.	B C D E F G A B
5. Lydian.	F G A B C D E F	6. Hypo-Lydian (or Ionian).	C D E F G A B C
7. Mixo-Lydian.	G A B C D E F G	8. Hypo-mixo-Lydian.	D E F G A B C D

On comparison it will be seen that the plagal modes commence at a fourth below the authentic. The above are known as the eight " Gregorian modes."

11. St. Gregory established a music school at which these modes and the order of the Church Service were systematically taught. The liturgy was noted entirely, it is said, by himself, and the whole was entitled the "Antiphonar," the chant or plain-song (*cantus-planus,* or *cantus-firmus*) being sung alternately or antiphonally

between priest and choir. A very crude description of notation was used, consisting of dots and scratches of various shapes, and the "stave" was then unknown.

12. The system founded by Gregory the Great quickly spread throughout the Christian countries. Trained teachers and singers were sent from Rome to France and Germany (604—752), and schools of Church music were established in most of the principal dioceses in those countries. It is, however, affirmed that the improvement effected was but transient, owing to the barbarous and untutored condition of the people, who in those times were little more than savages.

13. The Emperor **Charlemagne** (768—814) proved himself a zealous apostle of the musical system of St. Gregory. He founded music schools at Metz and other towns, and placed them under Italian singers of note. In this work the emperor employed one **Alcuin**, a British ecclesiastic, as his principal assistant, and Charlemagne himself paid periodical visits of inspection to these schools, both in France and Germany. It was not until this period that "Gregorians" became the universal use throughout western Christendom.

14. There is documentary evidence that at this period musicians had a crude conception of harmony. Isidore of Seville, a contemporary of Gregory, alludes in his "Treatise on Music" to Symphony and Diaphony, concerning which Professor Ritter observes—"By the first word he meant probably a combination of consonant, and by the latter of dissonant, intervals." Some little time after the death of Charlemagne, **Hucbald** (840—930), a Fleming, accompanied his melodies by a *discantus*, or added part, consisting of a series (when combined with the melody) of consecutive fourths or fifths; a "diaphony" which would be simply horrible in our ears. *Organum* was another term for this weird accompaniment. The organ was now in use at some churches, and in Winchester Cathedral there was an

instrument having 400 pipes, a magnificent one for those days.

15. **Guido of Arezzo** (990—1050) effected many important improvements in the system of notation, or rather founded the system upon which our present method is based.   The somewhat comprehensive term, *inventor musicæ*, was applied to him by the musicians of his time.   Hitherto two lines only had been employed as a stave ; to these he added two others.   Each of these additional lines had its distinctive colour—the one red, the other green or yellow.   The yellow line indicated the place of the note C ; the red line the place of the note F ;   and from these our C and F clefs are respectively derived.   Guido may also be regarded as the father of solmization, for he invented the terms *ut, re, mi, fa, sol, la,* which are used by students even now.   (*Si* was not used till the 17th century, when Lemaire introduced it as a name for the seventh of the scale, or leading note.) The terms used by Guido were derived from the following Latin lines, which he taught his students to sing to a melody so arranged that each line began with the note it was employed to indicate :—

UT queant laxis,	FAmuli tuorum,
REsonare fibris,	SOLve polluti
MIra gestorum,	LAbii reatum,
	Sancte Johannes.

16. **Franco of Cologne** (*c.* 1200) * formulated a system of musical measure and time by means of varying the shape of a note to denote its comparative length. They were named and figured as follows :—*maxima,* ▬▬

---

* Forkel assigns to Franco a much earlier date than this, maintaining that he flourished during the latter half of the 11th century.

(or *duplex longa*); *longa,* ▄▄ ; *brevis,* ■ ; and *semi-brevis,* ◆. He likewise invented " rests " of the same relative values, and the signs he used are practically identical with those of the present day. He divided time into " triple," or perfect, and " duple," or imperfect. The bar ≣, which gives a more perfect rhythm and accent to music, was not introduced till a much later date. In Franco's time, counterpoint of even five parts was employed in the accompaniment of melodies, but, although no longer restricted to progressions of fourths, fifths, and octaves, the harmony was of the most rigid kind, imperfect concords being at that period classed as discords.

17. **Adam de la Hale,** who also lived in the 13th century,* was a famous troubadour or wandering minstrel, and wrote songs in three-part harmony, the melodies of which would be accounted agreeable even in the present day. In character the songs of De la Hale are not unlike the popular " folk-songs " of Southern France and Northern Spain, as still sung by the rural population in those provinces. As in those early times Church music was exclusively in the hands of ecclesiastics, so these troubadours were the chief composers of secular music. As a rule they also wrote their own " words." Amongst the most notable troubadours were DE LA HALE, CHATELAIN DE COURCY, (King) THIBAUT of Navarre, and FAIDIT.

18. **Marchettus of Padua** (*c.* 13—), is credited with having " established the first correct principles in the use of consonances and dissonances ; " while to **Jean de Meurs** (*c.* 1330), who was probably a contemporary of Marchettus, is ascribed the introduction of florid counterpoint. It is supposed by some, that notwithstanding the character of the name, Jean de Meurs (or de Muris) was an Englishman.

---

* Czerny fixes the date at about 1280.

19. (**B**.) We now come to the rise of the Belgian School. About this time (14th century) Belgian musicians began to devote themselves in a special degree to the elaboration of counterpoint (harmony as a distinct branch of study was not known till long afterwards), and so distinguished themselves in the art that they won the best appointments in France and Germany.

20. (**B**.) The first important name in the Belgian series is that of **Guillaume Dufay** (1380—1430), chapelmaster (*maestro di cappella*) at Rome. He harmonized many existing melodies, both sacred and secular, in fairly good style, for four voices. He also wrote masses, in which appear some excellent specimens of canon. Dufay was followed by **Johannes Ockenheim** [or Ockeghem] (1430—1513), who has been called " the Sebastian Bach of the 15th century," and of whom some say that he founded the canonic or fugal style.* This latter assertion, as we have already seen, is scarcely true. As to canon we have positive evidence that Dufay was familiar with that form of writing, while in those days a " fugue " was scarcely more than a free style of canon. There is no doubt, however, that Ockenheim's work was more polished, and had more breadth and design ; but he fell, with his contemporaries, into the error of exhibiting his contrapuntal skill at the expense of the feeling of the music.

21. (**B**.) But both as a scholar and as a composer, Ockenheim was outdone by his brilliant contemporary and pupil, **Jusquin des Prés** (1440—1521), of whom Luther was wont to say that he was " master of notes, while others were mastered by notes." Various amusing anecdotes are told of Des Prés, who is accused of making musical puns in his compositions " to gain his private ends." It is more to our present purpose to record his originality as a composer ; for he was one of the first to discard the old *cantus firmus* and secular *motif*, and to

---

* '*Sumer is a cumen in*,' an English composition (*c.* 1250), is, however, an earlier instance of canonic writing.

invent his own musical subjects. Des Prés wrote
several masses and motetts, in four and in five parts.
He began his public career as a singer in the pope's
chapel, but subsequently became chapel-master to
Louis XII. of France. Des Prés numbered among his
pupils ARCADELDT, MOUTON, WILLAERT, GOUDIMEL,
CLEMENS non PAPA, and other excellent musicians.

22. (B.) **Adrian Willaert** (1490—1563) is frequently spoken of as "the founder of the Venetian
School." As, however, Willaert was a Belgian both by
birth and by training, it is confusing, if not altogether
misleading, to disconnect him from the Belgian School.
Indeed, we doubt if the existence of "the Venetian
School" is sufficiently distinct and apart from the
Belgian and Roman Schools to merit a separate page in
the annals of musical history. It is better, therefore, to
class the Venetian and Roman Schools (after the time
of Willaert) under the common head of "Italian."
Willaert received his training from Des Prés,—some say
from Mouton also,—and after many wanderings finally
settled at Venice, where eventually he obtained the
post of chapel-master at St. Mark's. Willaert was a
voluminous composer of songs and motetts, some of
which he arranged for two, even three, separate choirs ;
and to him is ascribed the introduction of a new
feature—the *madrigal.* He was succeeded at St. Mark's
by **Cyprian de Rore**, a pupil and fellow-countryman,
who became so popular with the Italians that they
styled him "Il divino." De Rore excelled in the
madrigal. Another contemporary of Willaert was **J.
Mouton**, master of the chapel to Francis I. of France.

23. (B.) The most distinguished contemporary of
Willaert was **Orlando Lassus**, or LATTRE (1520—
1595), who attempted nearly every then-known form
of composition, but devoted himself chiefly to Church
music, such as psalms, hymns, litanies, magnificats,
motetts, &c., &c. His settings of the Seven Penitential
Psalms, for five voices, are amongst his best works.

Lassus introduced the *chromatic* element into musical composition, as well as such musical terms as *Allegro* and *Adagio.* He was greatly eulogized in his day, was spoken of as "the prince of music" (*musicæ princeps*), and received the order of the Golden Spur.

24. (**B.**) With Lassus, the famous Belgian School is brought to a close. To the Belgians we owe a considerable development of the great first principles of the art; but they carried their scholasticisms too far, and burdened their music with painful elaborations and curious conceits. The spirit was lost in the letter. For material on which to build their numerous contrapuntal devices they indiscriminately selected Gregorian plainchants and secular melodies, even to love ditties and comic songs, which gave their titles to the masses and motetts that were built upon them; *e. g.* "The Noses Red," "Adieu, my loves," were well-known titles of sacred compositions. During this period the canonic or imitative form of counterpoint was developed; the madrigal, too, was introduced. It is *said* that BERNHARDT, a German, invented the organ pedal about the year 1490.* PETRUCCI, an Italian, was the inventor of movable music-types, 1502. For some time prior to this date music had been printed from large wooden blocks on which the characters were engraved.

25. (**E.**) We have now to speak of the Early English School, which, so far as we have any record, was inaugurated by **Dunstable**, who died in 1458. He has been called "the father of English contrapuntists," and was reputed as excellent a musician as his contemporary, Dufay. Another early writer was **John Taverner** (*c.* 1530), organist of Christ Church, Oxford. **Christopher Tye** (*c.* 1500—1560) in the year 1545 received the degree of Doctor in Music from the University of Cambridge. Tye was afterwards appointed organist of the Chapel Royal, and was the

---

* As organ pedals were in existence before this date, the truth probably is that Bernhardt introduced them about this time at Venice.

music-master of Queen Elizabeth, who prided herself on her playing of the Virginals,—a kind of primitive pianoforte, and the precursor of the latter instrument. Tye wrote a number of works, the best known amongst them in the present day being the anthem *I will exalt Thee, O Lord.*

26. (**E.**) The reign of Queen Elizabeth was prolific in musicians, as it was in authors, soldiers, and states-men. **John Merbecke** (1523—1585), first a singer, afterwards organist, of the Chapel Royal at Windsor, suffered many trials during the reign of Mary, on account of his profession of the reformed faith. It is even said that he narrowly escaped martyrdom. Mer-becke's principal work was the setting of the English Liturgy to a plain-song, which survives and is commonly used to this day. It was THOMAS TALLIS (1529—1585) who harmonized (and slightly altered) Merbecke's *cantus.* The skill of Tallis as a contrapuntist was unsur-passed by any of his contemporaries at home or abroad. He wrote a motett in no less than forty parts : of the art of canon he was a consummate master. His well-known "Evening Hymn," in which occurs an infinite canon at the octave between the treble and the tenor, is an ex-tract from a larger work. A notable pupil of Tallis was **William Byrde** (1543—1623), composer of the famous canon *Non Nobis Domine,* and one of the chief con-tributors to Queen Elizabeth's "Virginal Book"—a celebrated collection of studies for the Queen's favourite musical instrument. Other Church composers of this period were: **Richard Farrant** (*d.* 1580—1), whose reputed anthem, *Lord, for Thy tender mercies' sake,** is still a familiar composition ; **Robert White** (*d.* 1580); and **Dr. John Bull** (*d.* 1622), the first professor of music at Gresham College. It will be noticed that two

---

* Recently proved to be by Hilton. A service in G minor, however, still remains the undisputed work of Farrant.

great composers of this period died wi¹hin the same year (1585), namely, Merbecke and Tallis.

27. (**E.**) During the latter half of the 16th century the " madrigal " became exceedingly popular in this, as in other countries, and a number of English composers devoted their especial efforts to this form of composition. The madrigal may be briefly described as a part-song, of a light and generally a pastoral character (iii. 22). The principal madrigalists of this time were, **Thomas Morley, Kirbye, Dowland, Weelkes, Wilbye,** and **Benet.** The renowned collection entitled "The Triumphs of Oriana," to which, with Morley at their head, a number of composers contributed, was published in 1601. The book was dedicated to Queen Elizabeth.

28. (**I.**) We turn now to the rise of the purely Italian School, which is generally admitted to have been inaugurated by the compositions of **Constanzo Festa** (*d.* 1545), who, although trained in the school of the Belgians, rose above the mere scholasticisms and narrowing traditions of his predecessors. Festa was a member of the Sist¹ne choir at Rome, and wrote a number of Church compositions, of which a *Te Deum* has survived to this day. He also wrote madrigals.

29. (**I.**) But the chief glory of that period was **G. Palestrina** (1514—1594) who lived to effect a complete revolution in the style of musical composition for the Church. A pupil of **Goudimel** (1510—1572), himself a musician of no ordinary attainments, Palestrina is said to have " grasped the essential doctrines of Goudimel's school without adopting its mannerism." In 1562 occurred an event which brought Palestrina into noble prominence, as the leader, if not the originator, of a more exalted tone in sacred music, because more religious and devotional. In that year (1562) the famous Council of Trent expressed its condemnation of the frivolities that had so long crept into compositions of the most solemn character—such as the wholesale introduction of secular airs associated in the popular

mind with amorous or humorous words—and demanded
the restoration in their place of the old Gregorian plain-
chant. This sweeping edict was strongly resisted,
however, by Pope Pius IV., who prevailed upon the
Council to rest their decision upon a new work to be
composed for that purpose by Palestrina. Palestrina
undertook the commission, and in 1565 had completed
three masses, which, on their being performed before a
Commission of Cardinals, won for their composer the
distinction of having rescued Church music from a
threatened relapse into comparative barbarism. The
best of these three works was dedicated to the memory of
a former pope, who had been an early patron of Palestrina, and was called after his name (*Missa Papœ Marcelli*). During his long and brilliant career, Palestrina
composed numberless works, including several masses
—some of them in six parts,—a *Stabat Mater* for two
choirs, Lamentations, *Improperia*, and many motetts.
To Palestrina is attributed the transposition of the
cantus firmus or principal melody of a composition,
from the tenor part, where hitherto it had invariably
been placed, to the soprano or highest voice. Palestrina
was succeeded at Rome by FELICE ANERIO, who worthily
continued the work of reformation which Palestrina
had so well begun. We must not, however, omit to
mention **Nanini** (*d.* 1607) a contemporary and *collabora-
teur* of Palestrina, and moreover a gifted and thought-
ful writer. Nanini and Palestrina together instituted a
school in Rome in which the *nuova musica*, as it was
called, was carefully taught and faithfully continued.

30. (**I.**) Other notable contemporaries of Palestrina
were : **Christoforo Morales** (*b.* 1510), a Spaniard, who
in 1540 was admitted into the Sistine choir at Rome,
and wrote many compositions for the Church. His
motett for six voices, *Lamentabatur Jacobus*, is still
performed in the Sistine Chapel. **Luca Marenzio**
(1550—1594), called "the sweet swan," composed a
number of Church works, but especially distinguished

himself as a madrigalist. **Giuseppe Zarlino** (1519—1590), besides writing many elaborate Church compositions, published several works on Musical Theory. **Giovanni Gabrieli** (1540—1612), a nephew and pupil of A. GABRIELI (a great contrapuntist in his day), directed his chief attention to the improvement of compositions for combined choirs. He also made some crude attempts at orchestration ; amongst his works may be mentioned *In Ecclesiis Benedicite Domine* for two choirs, with accompaniments for one violin, three cornets, and two trombones ; also *Surrexit Christus*, for three voices, two violins, two cornets, and four trombones. **Tomaso Ludovico Vittoria** (1560—1608), a Spaniard, was another distinguished Church composer of this period. It will be seen that we have classed these Spanish musicians with the Italian School, as Spain never had, properly speaking, a distinctive school of her own.

31. (**B.**) The latest lights of the old Belgian School, which was now fast dying out, or rather was merging into the Italian School, were : **Jacques Arcadeldt** (1500 — 1570) ; **Jacques Clement** ("non Papa") (1500—1566) ; **Hubert Waelrant** (1517—1595), who made certain improvements in the art of solmization ; **Claude Lejeune** (1540 — 1600) ; all prolific and scholarly writers. Some of Arcadeldt's compositions are in use at the present day, and are highly esteemed by Church musicians.

32. (**I.**) ORIGIN OF THE OPERA. About the year 1580, we find a society of *literati* established in Florence with the object of instituting a revival of the ancient Greek art of musical and dramatic declamation. The *recitative* was thus introduced, in imitation of the intoned recitations of the old Greek tragedies. In 1594 was produced the first opera, entitled *Dafne*, the words by the poet Rinuccini, the music by **Peri**. In this work the *musica parlante*, or recitative, in a somewhat crude style, was first represented. The success of *Dafne*

called forth the opera *Euridice*, of which Peri and his friend **Caccini** were the joint composers. *Euridice* was produced on the occasion of the marriage of Mary de Medicis with Henri IV. of · France, at Florence, in the year 1600. But it was reserved for **Claudio Monteverde** (1566—1650) to give a pronounced form to the opera, and to impart to the recitative a more decided character. Monteverde was strongly condemned by his contemporaries for the unprecedented licence of his harmonies, as well as for the freedom of his melody. It is said that Monteverde was the first to employ the chord of the dominant seventh without preparation. His principal operas were *Orfeo, Arianna, Il Ballo delle Ingrate*, and *Tancred and Clorinde*. The orchestras of this period were of the most primitive kind, consisting of one or two flutes, lutes, viols, and a harpsichord or spinet, the players generally being placed behind the scenes. The further progress of opera will be traced in subsequent pages of this work.

33. (I.) THE RISE OF ORATORIO. The development of the oratorio progressed side by side with that of the opera. For ages it had been the custom on important ecclesiastical occasions to perform " miracle-plays," or rude—we might say profane—dramas on sacred subjects. About the middle of the 16th century, St. Philip de Neri, a priest of Florence, devoted himself to the improvement of these performances, and introduced historical scenes or sacred allegories in the course of the services he held in his *oratory*. (Hence the term *Oratorio*, which is the Italian for " oratory.") The first oratorio worthy the name was not produced till the year 1600, when *L'Anima e corpo*, by EMILIO DEL CAVALIERE, was performed at a church in Rome. The composer arranged his accompaniments for the following instruments : a double lyre, a harpsichord, a double guitar (or *theorbo*) and two flutes. What Monteverde did, however, for the opera, was effected for oratorio by **Giacomo Carissimi** (1580 — 1673), who made many

improvements in the existing form of the recitative, and invented the *Arioso*, from which sprang the more elaborated *Aria*. His best known works are *Jephtha* and *Jonah ;* the latter oratorio was revived a few years ago by Mr. Henry Leslie, whose celebrated choir has given some excellent performances of the work.

34. (I.) The most noted Italian composers of this period were : **Ludovico Viadana** (1560—1625), who is said to have composed " the first Church concertos and solo songs for the Church." He was also the first to write harmony as distinguished from pure counter-point, and accompanied his voices (generally on the organ) from a *basso continuo*, or figured bass. Whether he actually invented the " figured bass " is, however, a matter of some doubt : it is said to have been employed in the first instance by Catalano (*b.* 1595), a Sicilian. Viadana's tenor solo *Bone·Jesu*, had an accompani-ment of two trombones—an odd combination, truly, as it would seem to our more sensitive ears. **Gregorio Allegri** (1580—1652) was another active writer for the Church : his best known composition is a *Miserere*, which is still performed at the " Sistine," and at other Roman Churches. In 1877 this composition was sung (for the first time, we believe, in an Anglican Church) at All Saints', Margaret Street, under the direction of Mr. W. Stevenson Hoyte, the organist. **Orazio Benevoli** (*d.* 1672) wrote several famous motetts, some of which are scored for as many as 24 voices with brass accom-paniments. **Geronimo Frescobaldi** (1587—1654) wrote a number of fugues, madrigals, and Church composi-tions, and was regarded in his day as a very accomplished organist.

35. (G.) The German, as a distinctive school, sprang from, and grew up with, the great Protestant movement under **Luther** (1483—1546), which began about 1524 Luther introduced the *Chorale*, from which our modern hymn-tune is undoubtedly derived, and to Luther himself are attributed several fine compositions of this

order. In 1524 a collection of chorales by **J. Walther** (1490—1555), a friend of Luther, was published at Wittemberg, under the immediate supervision of Luther himself. Luther obtained compositions of the same kind from Goudimel and Clemens non Papa, already mentioned. **Johann Eccard** (*b. circa* 1545), **Ludwig Senfl** (1490—1560), **Lucas Lossius** (1508—1582), **Jacobus Gallus**, or **Händl** (1550—1591), amongst whose works is a motett in twenty-four parts, for four choirs. **Melchior Vulpius** (1560—1616), **Leo Hassler** (1564—1618), **M. Praetorius** (1571—1621), were all eminent musicians of this school and period. But especial mention must be made of **Heinrich Schütz** (1585—1672) who has been called the "Father of German Oratorio." He wrote *The Passion* according to the four Evangelists, the *Story of the Resurrection of our Lord*, and *Seven Last Words*. Schütz also composed the first German opera, *Daphne* (set to a German translation of Rinuccini's words), which was performed at Dresden, 1627.

36. (**E.**) Reverting to the English School, the next important name is that of **Orlando Gibbons** (1583—1625), who was born at Cambridge, and received his musical training at the Chapel Royal, of which he was appointed organist at the age of 21. Gibbons attained to a leading position amongst his contemporaries, was a great favourite with Charles I., and was admitted a Doctor of Music at the University of Oxford. Many of his Church compositions are in use at this day—notably the anthem *Hosanna to the Son of David*, and the well-known Church Service in F. **Henry Lawes** (1600—1662) was a prolific and highly-favoured writer—chiefly of secular compositions—and set to music several "masques" (the private theatricals of those times), the best known among which is Milton's *Comus*. **William Child** (1608—1696) is another composer of this period whose music may even now be heard in our churches. **Matthew Lock** (1620—1677)

is chiefly remembered through the famous "Macbeth music," which, however, is more probably a work of Purcell's. But he wrote a number of works, sacred as well as secular. His opera *Psyche*, produced in 1673, was the first English opera, properly so called, and was also, as we believe, the first opera presented on an English stage. Another opera composer of this period was John Eccles (*b. circa* 1620), but his works have not survived him. John Blow (1648—1708) wrote some excellent anthems, of which *I was in the Spirit, I beheld, and lo*, are the best known. Michael Wise (*d.* 1687) has also given some lasting contributions to Church music.

37. (E.) Henry Purcell (1658—1695) has with justice been styled "the greatest English musical genius." A pupil of Dr. Blow, and chorister in the King's Chapel, Purcell had the inestimable advantage of a sound and early training. At the early age of 18 he was appointed organist of Westminster Abbey, and in 1677, a year later, he composed his first opera, *Dido and Æneas*. This work made at once a foremost place for him among the composers of his time, and in 1690 another opera, *The Tempest*, set to words by Dryden, added still further to Purcell's reputation as a dramatic composer. Amongst other operas by Purcell may be mentioned *King Arthur, Diocletian, Fairy Queen, Timon of Athens, Don Quixote*, and *The Libertine*. His music to the masque in the Tragedy of *Œdipus* must not be forgotten. The celebrated 12 sonatas for the violin, including the one called "The Golden Sonata," were composed in 1683. Almost the last work of Purcell was the *Te Deum* and *Jubilate* in D, with instrumental accompaniments, recently performed in St. Paul's Cathedral, at a festival of the College of Organists. Purcell was also an accomplished writer for the harpsichord, and indeed scarcely any then-known form of composition was left by him untried. He died at the early age of 37, and was honoured with a tomb in

Westminster Abbey. **Jer. Clark** (*d.* 1707), another
pupil of Dr. Blow, and a contemporary of Purcell, wrote
cathedral music which is still performed. The well-
known anthem, *I will love Thee, O Lord*, is perhaps
one of his best works. **Dr. Aldrich** (1647—1710),
Dean of Christ Church, Oxford, did much to encourage
musical art in his day, and was himself a prolific
composer of Church Services and anthems. With his
name we close the record of English musicians of the
17th century.

38. (**E.**) **William Croft** (1677—1727) has given the
Church some noble anthems, exceedingly popular even
now, amongst which may be mentioned *God is gone
up ; O Lord, Thou hast searched me out,*—for three
voices ;—*O Lord, rebuke me not,* in which there is a
fugue in six parts ; and *Put me not to rebuke.* In
1715 Croft was made a Doctor of Music at Oxford.
Maurice Greene (1698—1755) wrote some English
operas, now quite forgotten, and many Church compositions. **James Kent** (1700—1736) was a pupil and
great admirer and imitator of Croft. His anthems
Hear my Prayer, and *O Lord our Governor*, are among
the most popular at the present day. **J. Weldon**
(1708—1736), whose anthem *Hear my Crying* gives
evidence of the writer's skill and originality as a
harmonist, has left behind him work only sufficient to
cause lasting regret at his untimely death. **William
Boyce** (1710—1779) was eminent as an organist, and
wrote many organ pieces that were much admired in
his day, but he is now known chiefly by his numerous
vocal compositions. He wrote one opera, *The Chaplet*,
and one oratorio, *Solomon* (which by the way he terms
a *serenata*). His best known anthems are, *By the
waters of Babylon, The Lord is King,* and *O where
shall Wisdom.* He took the degree of Mus.D. at Cambridge in 1749. **Thomas Arne** (1710—1778) wrote as
many as 23 operas, three oratorios, and a great number
of anthems and songs. **John Travers** (*d.* 1758) is

another Church writer of this period; his anthem
Ascribe unto the Lord, for two voices, is a favourite
composition in our cathedral choirs. He also wrote
some canzonets, or short songs, for one and two voices.
James Nares (1715—1783) is the author of some 26
anthems. His Service in F is frequently sung in our
churches, and is likely to continue popular for many
years, as it is at once simple and melodious. **Jonathan
Battishill** (1738—1801) wrote several operas, and
many anthems, the latter including the celebrated composition for seven voices, *Call to Remembrance.* **Samuel
Arnold** (1739—1802) wrote 40 English operas and
seven oratorios, besides many Church compositions.
Perhaps his continuation of Boyce's Church Service in
A is the best known of all his works.

39. (**G**.) There would seem to exist, in the German
School, the want of a definite link between Schütz and
Bach; but Professor Ritter mentions one JOHN SEBAS-
TIANI (*circa* 1660), who appears to fill the gap. Sebastiani wrote a version of the *Passion* which was produced in 1672, the year in which Schütz died. This
work contains, we are told, a number of chorales
arranged in good counterpoint, interspersed with tenor
recitatives, all accompanied by strings. From this
description there is little doubt that Bach based the
form of his own *Passion-music* upon that of Sebastiani.
Reinhard Keiser (1673—1739), a native of Leipsic,
besides composing more than 100 operas, wrote "*The
Bleeding and Dying Jesus,*" an oratorio which he produced at Hamburg in 1704. In this work, however,
the usual recitations and chorales were omitted.

40. (**G**.) JOHANN SEBASTIAN BACH (1685—1750),
born of a race of musicians, was the son of J. A.
Bach, organist of Eisenach. At an early age, and
close upon the death of his father, he began his musical training under the care of his elder brother, J.
Christopher Bach, who also died when Sebastian was
but fourteen, leaving him without friends or means.

Bach, having a fine treble voice, entered a choir in Lüneberg, where he remained—long after he had lost his voice—until his eighteenth year, when he managed to obtain a place amongst the violinists in the Court band of the Duke of Saxe-Weimar. Shortly afterwards he was appointed organist at Arnstadt, and during the five years he held this position gave much time to self-improvement both in composition and in playing. In 1708 Bach removed to Weimar as Court organist, and his reputation both as organist and harpsichord player now rapidly spread through the surrounding States. In 1723 he was appointed to the directorship of the Thomas-Schule at Leipsic, a post which he held until his death. In 1725, Bach had completed the first volume of his *Wohltemperirte Klavier* (well-tempered Clavier) — the well-known forty-eight preludes and fugues. This work was not completed till the year 1740. His greatest works, the *Passion* according to St. John, and that of St. Matthew, were produced in 1729. A third *Passion*-oratorio, St. Luke, has also been attributed to Bach, but the authorship is held to be somewhat apocryphal. The Matthew-*Passion* is undoubtedly Bach's finest work : the dramatic double choruses, the expressive solos with their occasional obbligato accompaniments for instruments, the exquisitely harmonized chorales, proclaim alike his scholarship, his genius, and his unfeigned piety. The *Christmas Oratorio*, a smaller work, but containing many characteristic beauties, was produced in 1734. It is said that the *Christmas Oratorio* was originally intended for performance in six portions on six separate occasions during Christmastide. Bach's writings are numerous and varied in character. His mass in B minor (for although a zealous Protestant he wrote several masses), composed in 1733, has recently been performed in this country. His *suites des pièces* for the harpsichord will always form valuable studies for pianoforte-players. The *Suites Anglaises*, composed at the request of an

English amateur, rank among the best of Bach's efforts
in this style of composition. The celebrated *Art of
Fugue* (1749) was among the last of Bach's works, and
was written shortly before his blindness. Two of
Bach's sons, FRIEDEMANN BACH (1710—1784) and C.
PHILIPP EMANUEL BACH (1713—1788), were well-
esteemed musicians in their time. The latter in his
Instruction Book for playing the clavichord (1753)
introduced a new system of "fingering," which was
soon generally adopted. (iii. 37.)

41. (G.) GEORGE FREDERICK HANDEL (1685—1759)
was originally intended for the legal profession, but
evinced, at a very early age, a strong predilection for
music, and practised upon the harpsichord for some
time in secret. When he was about seven years old he
accompanied his father on a visit to the Court of the
Duke of Saxe-Weissenfels, and there accidentally found
an opportunity of playing upon the organ in the ducal
chapel. The duke was struck by the child's performance, and at length persuaded the father to devote his
son to the art as a profession. Handel was at once
placed under the care of Frederick Zachau, cathedral
organist at Halle, Handel's native town. Four years
afterwards he went to Berlin, where he first met his
future rival, Bononcini. Very shortly, however, his
father recalled him to Halle, having declined an offer
to send the youth to Italy for the purpose of complet-
ing his studies. On the death of his father, Handel
went to Hamburg as a violinist in the opera house.
Here he composed and produced his first opera, *Almira*,
1705. This was rapidly followed by other successful
operas—*Nero*, *Florinda*, and *Daphne*—all in the same
year. In 1706 Handel went to Florence, and at once
established his reputation there by the production of
Roderigo. He removed thence to Venice, and the opera
Agrippina made him very popular with the Venetians.
At Rome, Handel's first oratorio, *The Resurrection*, was
written and performed; and at Naples, the pastoral,

Aci Galatea e Polifemo, from which latter work his later cantata, *Acis and Galatea,* was in part derived. On his return to Germany, in 1710, Handel was appointed chapel-master to the Elector of Hanover. The same year he visited England ; and in 1711 *Rinaldo* was produced at the Haymarket with extraordinary success. After a short absence in Hanover, Handel returned to England, and composed (1713) the well-known *Utrecht Te Deum* and *Jubilate,* which was sung in St. Paul's cathedral, the queen (Anne) being present. On the succession of the Elector of Hanover to the throne of England (1714) Handel had cause to be apprehensive of the consequences of his neglect of the chapel-mastership at Hanover, and, it is said, composed the *Water Music* with a view to appeasing the wrath of his sovereign. However, he regained the favour of George I., and retained it as long as that monarch lived. Handel's oratorio on the *Passion* was written in Hanover in the year 1717, but was first performed at Hamburg. In the same year he was appointed director of the music at the chapel of the Duke of Chandos, who resided at Cannons. The celebrated *Chandos Te Deums and Anthems* were composed here. In 1720, an attempt was made to revive Italian Opera in London, and an association of persons, under the title of the Royal Academy of Music (not to be confounded with the existing institution of that name), was formed to promote the scheme, with Handel as musical director and composer. The first opera was *Radamistus,* and its success was complete. Handel's first English oratorio, *Esther,* was composed in the same year, and produced at Cannons ; and in 1721 the new *Acis and Galatea* was performed. About this time there was a serious division amongst the directors of the Haymarket opera, and Bononcini and Attilio were brought over from Germany in opposition to Handel. These circumstances ultimately led to the dissolution of the society, in 1728. For this opera, Handel wrote *Muzio Scævola,*

Floridante, Otho, Giulio Cesare, Flavius (where occurs the *Doni pace*) *Rodelinda, Scipio, Alexander, Admætus,* and *Ptolemy.* In 1729, he organized a new opera company, and wrote *Lothario, Parthenope, Porus, Ætius, Sosarme,* and *Orlando ;* but the enterprise proved a failure. Upon this Handel had recourse to oratorio, and in 1732 revived *Esther,* the success of which led to the performance of *Acis and Galatea.* This was followed by *Deborah* (1733). In this year Handel visited Oxford, where he produced *Athaliah,* and in consequence of its success was offered the degree of Doctor in Music, which, however, he declined. For the next two or three years Handel again busied himself with opera, and was again unsuccessful : during this period *Semiramis, Arbaces, Ariadne, Pastor Fido, Dido, Berenice,* and *Xerxes* were produced, as well as *Alexander's Feast,* the only successful work of this series. For a time Handel now gave his attention to the renowned organ-concertos, which give abundant proof of his exceptional skill as an organist. In 1738 the oratorio *Saul* was written, and in 1739 it was produced and most favourably received, at the Haymarket. *Israel in Egypt* was commenced immediately after the completion of *Saul,* which it followed at the Haymarket; then came *The Ode on St. Cecilia's Day.* The 12 grand concertos for harpsichord and strings appeared the same year, while shortly afterwards (in 1740), *L'Allegro ed Il Penseroso* was produced ; these failed at the first performance. Handel's great masterpiece, *The Messiah,* composed in 1741, and rejected in London, was performed at Dublin in 1742 and received with the greatest enthusiasm. *The Messiah* was followed by *Samson,* 1743 ; * *Belshazzar,* 1744 ; *Hercules,* 1744 ; *Joseph,* 1744 ; *Judas Maccabæus,* 1747 ; *Joshua,* 1747 ; *Solomon,* 1748 ; *Theodora,* 1749 ; *Susanna,* 1749 ; *Jephtha,* 1751. The *Dettingen Te Deum* dates

---

* In *Samson* the *Dead March* in *Saul* reappears.

1743. During the last seven or eight years of his life Handel was afflicted with total blindness. He died on Good Friday, 1759, and was buried in Westminster Abbey. Many of his smaller works have not been mentioned, but an exception must be made in the case of the *Suites*, in which *The Harmonious Blacksmith* is included.

42. (**G.**) Among the more conspicuous German contemporaries of Bach and Handel, Hasse and Graun deserve especial mention. **J. A. Hasse** (1699—1783), whom the Italians honoured as " the divine Saxon," excelled both in oratorio and in opera. But (**I.**) the writings of Hasse were all more or less formed upon Italian models, and therefore should properly be classed as belonging to the Italian School. Schlüter tells us that " of Hasse, a grand and noble *Te Deum*, as well as a *Requiem* (according to Krause, superior even to Mozart's), are still annually performed in the Catholic Court Church at Dresden. On the other hand, the light Italian style and opera air appear without disguise or reticence in his masses and oratorios." **C. H. Graun** (1701—1759) is now chiefly remembered through his great " passion" work, *Der Tod Jesu* (The Death of Jesus), which has recently been revived in Germany, and also in this country. **J. A. Hiller** (1728—1804) composed a number of light operas or operettas, including the celebrated *Liederspiele*. **Georg Benda** (1722—1795) was another prolific writer of opera ; *Ariadne auf Naxos* and *Medea* are his principal works. Mozart was greatly impressed with the beauty of *Medea*, which he heard during his visit to Mannheim in 1778. In the course of his observations on this melodrama, Mozart writes :— " It is not sung, but declaimed, and the music is like a recitative *obbligato ;* sometimes there is talking amid the music, which has a splendid effect." **J. G. Naumann** (1741—1801) principally devoted himself to Church music : his *Das Vater Unser*, a setting of Klopstock's paraphrase of the Lord's Prayer, is his

chief composition. **F. H. Himmel** (1765—1814) was a popular composer of opera, his *Fanchon* being among the most successful of his works.

43. (I.) **Alessandro Scarlatti** (1659—1725) gave to the oratorio a more decided form than it had at the hands of Carissimi and his contemporaries. He introduced independent movements (*intermezzi*) for the orchestra, which he greatly improved, and divided the aria into three distinct portions. He wrote masses, oratorios, operas, and other compositions; and his celebrated fugue for two choirs *Tu es Petrus*, is still occasionally performed at St. Peter's in Rome. His son, DOMENICO SCARLATTI, was a popular harpsichord player and composer for that instrument. **F. Durante** (1684—1755) wrote exclusively for the Church, in which branch of the art he did good service, but his claim to a place in musical history rests chiefly upon his having been the master of several musicians of eminence, including **F. Feo**, who composed, *inter alia*, a grand mass for two choirs (**A. Stradella**, composer of several fine oratorios, among them *St. John the Baptist*, is also accounted one of Durante's pupils, though there is apparently some evidence to the contrary); **Duni, Terradeglias, Jomelli** (1714—1774), and **Piccini**, hereafter mentioned. An important contemporary of Durante was **Leonardo Leo** (1694—1746), whose oratorio, *The Death of Abel*, is highly spoken of by historians. Other Italian or Neapolitan musicians of this period were **G. P. Pergolesi** (1710—1736), composer of a *Stabat Mater* and several operas; **G. Sacchini** (1735—1786); **Guglielmi, Galuppi, Lotti** (1660—1740), who adopted the then modern style in his operas; **A. Caldara** (1674—1763), one of the greatest masters of fugue; **Marcello** (1680 —1739), author of the *Paraphrases on the* 50 *Psalms of David.*

44. (FRENCH OPERA.) Originally an offshoot of the early Italian Opera, which was introduced into France by Cardinal Mazarin, about the year 1645, the French

School of Opera boasts a numerous array of composers. The first genuine French work was *La Pastorale*, composed (in 1659) by **R. Cambert**. But the actual founder of the French school was **J. B. Lully** (1633—1687), who, though by birth an Italian, was brought up in the household of the French monarch (Louis XIV.) and was placed in the king's private band as a violinist. His *Tragédies lyriques* consisted mainly of recitatives and choruses ; here he generally ignored the aria and the duet, both so highly characteristic of the Italian School. Lully is regarded as the originator of the overture, which he generally composed in two parts—the first an adagio, or slow movement, the second a sprightly minuet, or a fugue. Lully was succeeded by **J. P. Rameau** (1683—1764), the renowned mathematician and writer on musical theory, who greatly improved upon Lully's style, by introducing a greater variety in the melody and harmony of his vocal writings. His principal opera, *Castor and Pollux*, was a popular work with the French for many years, despite the strictures of ROUSSEAU, who complained that Rameau's harmonies were far-fetched, and destructive of tune. An attempt was made recently—in Paris—to effect a revival of *Castor and Pollux*, but the writer is not aware whether it was successful. During the lifetime of Rameau (1752), a rival opera company, imported from Italy, caused no small stir amongst French musicians. This company, whom the French styled " *Les Bouffons*," introduced a species of comic operetta, or *opera-bouffe*, on the French stage : but in a short time *Les Bouffons* were compelled to leave the country, through the persistent opposition of the French or " National " party. But they had left behind them the taste for *opera-bouffe*, and several French composers produced, almost immediately upon the departure of the Italians, a number of comic operettas—amongst them, *Les Troqueurs*, by D'AUVERGNE (1713—1797). Among other contemporaries of Rameau, were DUNI

(1709—1775), PHILIDOR, and MONSIGNY (1729—1817),
the composer of *Le Déserteur*, and *Rose et Colas*.
These paved the way for **Gretry** (1741—1813), in
whose reign the French operetta reached its zenith.
Despite the example of his great predecessor Rameau,
Gretry had recourse to the developed *aria* form, which
he frequently introduced in connection with the recitatives.   Gretry's *Richard Cœur-de-Lion* and *Zémire et
Azor* achieved for their writer an immense popularity
in his own day, and they have both been performed in
Paris in recent years.   Among the most favoured contemporaries of Gretry were : **D'Alayrac** (1753—1809),
composer of *Nina* and *Les deux Savoyards*—both lately
revived ; **Berton** (1766—1844), composer of *Montano
et Stephanie, Ponce de Léon, Le Délire, Aline,* and other
works of a similar character ; **Simon Catel** (1773—
1830), whose opera *Sémiramis* has been placed on
the French boards very lately ; and lastly, **Nicolo
Isouard** (1777—1818), a native of Malta, composer of
the much-admired *Cendrillon.* These names, with those
of BOIELDIEU, GOSSEC, and MEHUL, the celebrated author
of *Joseph*, bring us down almost to the present generation
of French composers.

45. (I.) CH. W. GLUCK (1714—1787), a native of
Bohemia, received his training at Prague and Vienna ;
and subsequently at Milan, where he studied Italian
opera under Samartini.   In 1741, his first opera *Ar-
taxerxes* was produced at Milan, and its success encouraged him to write *Clytemnestra* and *Demetrio*,
which were produced at the same theatre.   In 1745,
Gluck visited England, and his *Caduta del Giganti*
and *Artamene* were produced at the Haymarket, with,
however, but doubtful success.   After a few years' stay
in this country, Gluck returned to Vienna, and thence
went to Rome, where, in 1754, *La Clemenza di Tito a
Antigone* were well received.   He afterwards went to
Florence, and the real importance of this visit consists
in the valuable friendship which Gluck then formed

with the poet Calzabigi, whose schemes for the improvement of opera were cordially entered into by the composer. The result was the production in 1764 * of *Orfeo*, at Vienna, on the occasion of the marriage of the Emperor Joseph II. In *Orfeo*, the drama is released from the old restraints and conceits with which Italian opera had too long been burdened, and the music was written with a view to heightening the dramatic effect of the work. The opera met with an unqualified success, and fully established Gluck in the front rank of composers. This work was followed, in 1767, by *Alceste*, which was a further development of the same art principles. This work, however, was not so well received as the composer had reason to expect, and in his disappointment he turned to Paris. (46.)

46. (F.) GLUCK arrived in Paris in 1773, and early in 1774 *Iphigénie en Aulide* was performed, and ultimately gained him his footing in the French capital. He subsequently adapted to the French stage his *Orfeo* and *Alceste*. The advent in Paris of a formidable rival, **Piccini** (1728—1800), who sought to establish in France the old and exploded form of Italian opera, created some sensation, and aroused considerable party feeling. This occurred in 1776. The musical world in Paris was split into two powerful parties, the "Gluckists" and the "Piccinists," and the controversy was carried on with a good deal of unnecessary acrimony. In 1777 Gluck produced *Armide* · which, however, suffered a temporary eclipse by the production in the following year of Piccini's *Roland*. Gluck's *Iphigénie en Tauride*, however, in 1779, practically asserted his triumph, although the rivalry continued until his death in 1787.

47. (G.) JOSEPH HAYDN (1732—1809) was born

---

* Some writers give 1762 as the date of *Orfeo*, while *Alceste* has been assigned to the years 1766, 1767, and 1769 respectively.

of poor parents, in the village of Rohrau, on the Austrian frontier. His first step in a long musical career was in the capicity of a chorister in the Cathedral of St. Stephen, at Vienna, not many miles from his native place. Here he remained eight years, and during this period received lessons on the violin and harpsichord from the cathedral choir-master, Reuter. It is said that Haydn practised at least sixteen hours a day. His first lessons in composition were obtained, not from Reüter, but from Fux's *Gradus ad Parnassum*, which he studied without the help of a master. On quitting, when his voice had broken, the cathedral choir, Haydn suffered a good deal of privation, and scraped together a scanty living by means of harpsichord lessons. After some rebuffs, he obtained the position of personal attendant upon Nicolo Porpora, a popular singing-master of that day, who allowed Haydn the privilege of playing the accompaniments during the singing lessons, and eventually gave him a good deal of valuable instruction in singing and composition. While thus engaged, Haydn contrived to secure one or two poorly paid appointments, such as the choir-mastership of a church in Vienna, the organistship of a private chapel, and the position of tenor singer in the Cathedral of St. Stephen. About the year 1750, when he was 18 or 19, Haydn obtained his first introduction to the public through the instrumentality, it is said, of one Curtz, a comic actor, who commissioned him to compose an opera, *The Devil on Two Sticks*. This was represented at one of the Vienna theatres, and had a short-lived success. Haydn next devoted himself to the composition of instrumental trios and other chamber music, which at once made him popular, notwithstanding the opposition he met with from certain quarters on account of supposed musical heresies. His reputation as a youthful composer of promise brought him to the notice of Prince Esterházy, an enthusiastic amateur, who, struck with the merit and originality of a new symphony of Haydn's, retained the composer in his private service; subsequently (1760) giving him the appointment of chapel-master—a post which he continued to hold till the death of the prince, in 1790. During his tenure of office, Haydn composed a large number of symphonies, operas, masses, concertos, trios, quartets, and other vocal and instrumental works. In 1790 he was induced, on the earnest representations of Salomon, to visit London, where Salomon acted as director of the " Professional Concerts," the scheme of which was very similar to that of the present " Philharmonic Concerts." Under agreement, Haydn produced either a symphony or a smaller composition at each concert given by Salomon. The success of this professional campaign induced Haydn to revisit London (in 1794), where he remained until the May of the following year. During his two visits he composed the group known as the *London Symphonies*, twelve in number, which rank amongst the finest of his orchestral works. On his return to Vienna, he retired from professional and public life, but still busied himself in composition, and in 1798—at the age of 66—produced his great oratorio, *The Creation*. This work, the words for which, it is said, were originally written (by Lidley) for Handel, produced a profound impression at the first performance, which took place in the Schwartzenberg Palace, Vienna. The fame of *The Creation* soon spread through Europe; in England it has long been second only to *The Messiah* in popular favour. Thomson's well-known poem furnished the subject for Haydn's next oratorio, *The Seasons*, which was completed in 1801. This was Haydn's last important work. A complete list of his compositions would fill two or three pages of this book; they have, however, been summarized as follows :—" Symphonies, 118; quartets, 83; concertos, 24; trios, 24; sonatas, 44; operas, 19; masses, 15; dances, about 400; pieces for the baryton (a species of *viol-da-gamba*), 163;" but this summary is by no means

exhaustive. In oratorio, besides *The Creation* and *The
Seasons*, must be mentioned *The Return of Tobias;* and
lastly, *The Seven Last Words*—a beautiful but little-
known work, lately revived. (*The Seven Last Words*
was performed in the church of St. Peter, Bayswater,
on Good Friday, 1876, and again in 1877, under the
direction of Mr. Edwin Lott, organist of the church.)
Haydn is generally regarded as the founder of the
modern symphony, and the sonata-form ; but he himself has acknowledged his indebtedness in these respects to Philipp Emanuel Bach, "who first prepared
the way for the brilliant epoch of instrumental music
which began with Haydn." The latter may, nevertheless, be regarded as the father of modern orchestration.

48. (G.) **Wolfgang Amadeus Mozart** (1756 —
1791), the son of Leopold Mozart,—himself an excellent musician, and author of a treatise on the violin
—was born at Salzburg, Germany. At a very early age
Mozart gave surprising tokens of his musical genius,
which the father fostered and encouraged in every possible way. At the age of four years he received his
first lessons on the harpsichord, and two or three years
afterwards on the violin. It is narrated that when he
was only six years old he made his first crude attempt
at musical composition—a concerto for the clavier—
which was not devoid of distinct musical idea and
expression. About this time his father took the boy
and his sister Maria—the latter eleven years old—on a
professional tour to Vienna, where they were received
with much favour, and were invited to perform before
the Emperor and Empress. The following year they
visited Munich, Mayence, and other cities of Southern
Germany, and thence proceeded to Paris and London.
In London they performed before the King and Queen
(George III. and Charlotte) at St. James's. Everywhere
the little musicians—more, probably, by reason of their
youth than for their actual performances—were petted
and caressed. In 1765 they went to Holland, where

young Mozart wrote the six sonatas, for violin with piano-forte or harpsichord accompaniment, for the Princess of Orange. Early in 1767 Mozart went again to Vienna, where he spent two or three years in study and compo-sition. Here, besides writing two or three small operas and a *Stabat Mater*, he produced his first mass, on a commission from the Emperor, in 1768. In 1770 he commenced a lengthy and eventful tour through Italy, receiving much praise and many honours and keep-sakes, but very little pecuniary reward. His opera, *Mitridate*, was performed at Milan during this tour; but although it had a temporary success, this opera does not deserve a legitimate place in any catalogue of Mozart's compositions. His next opera, *La Finta Giar-diniera*, produced at Munich in 1775, in many respects shows a sensible advance upon previous work, but con-tains no features worthy of special comment. His first really important opera is *Idomeneo*, which was produced at Munich in 1781. This work, although to a great extent built upon the old Italian model, especially with respect to the elaborated *aria*, abounds in characteristic beauties, both in the choruses and in the instrumental scoring. Owing to the weakness of the libretto, and its want of dramatic interest, it is ineligible for the modern opera-stage. Occasional excerpts, however, are still to be heard in the concert-room. *Die Entführung aus dem Serail*, produced the following year, exhibits a growing independence of style, and more varied re-sources in the illustration of the several contrasting characters. *Le Nozze di Figaro* (1786) is too well known to be commented upon here; we may, however, note that this is Mozart's finest work from the purely dramatic point of view; while *Don Giovanni* (1787) excels in the elucidation of individual character. Respecting the latter work, a German critic writes: " Mozart's *Don Giovanni* is, by its marvellous delinea-tion of both the lights and shadows of life, its com bined seriousness and playfulness, tragedy and comedy

a universal, unique, and deeply significant work ; one
to which, in the sister art of drama, Goethe's *Faust* can
alone be worthily compared." The succeeding opera,
Cosi fan tutte (1790), though containing many inci-
dental beauties, is marred by the childish and essentially inartistic character of the libretto. In 1791
appeared *La Clemenza di Tito,*—the libretto of which
is identical with that previously employed by Gluck
and others—which was performed at Prague for the
coronation of the Emperor Leopold II. In this opera
Mozart introduced (to the *aria, Non piu di fiori*) an
obbligato for a new instrument, the Corno de bassetto, or
basset-horn, a kind of low clarionet, now practically
obsolete. Two of these " basset-horns " are also employed in the *Requiem,* of which we shall have to
speak later on. In many of the details of *La Clemenza
di Tito* Mozart had recourse to the assistance of his
pupil, Süssmaier, who, it is said, wrote most of the
recitatives for this opera. Within a few weeks of the
production of *Tito,* the *Zauberflöte* (*Il Flauto Magico*)
was completed, and performed at Vienna, and was
repeated one hundred times during the same and the
following year. This was his last opera. Mozart had
also been active in the production of other works. He
had written many masses, and several symphonies, of
which the finest are the G minor, the E flat, and the
Jupiter Symphony in C, besides numerous quartets, and
other chamber music. He had also written a number
of pianoforte concertos and sonatas (which latter are
seldom performed in public). His last work was the
Requiem (1791), the greater portion of which he composed on his death-bed. There has been much discussion among critics regarding the authenticity of three
important numbers in this beautiful work. It is
asserted by some that the pupil, Süssmaier, who had
already given Mozart much assistance in the preparation
of *La Clemenza di Tito* and other contemporaneous or
later works, actually composed the greater part of

the *Requiem.* If this be the case, it is surprising how Süssmaier sustained the individuality of Mozart throughout the remainder of the work, and it is still more astonishing that, apart from his connection with Mozart, so accomplished a writer should have left behind him no other abiding memorial of his own powers. The numbers claimed by Süssmaier as having been entirely composed by himself are the three last— *Sanctus, Benedictus,* and *Agnus Dei.* Mozart's wonderful skill in orchestration has been exemplified to us not only in his own works. The originally thin scoring of *The Messiah* was expanded by him in 1789, and since then Mozart's "additional accompaniments" have invariably been adopted at the performances of this oratorio. Other works of Handel were similarly re-scored by Mozart. As a contrapuntist, also, Mozart takes high rank. The fugal movement (finale) in the *Jupiter Symphony,* and that in the overture to *Zauber-flöte,* are standard examples of the highest form of contrapuntal development.

49. (**G.**) The German contemporaries of Haydn and Mozart are very numerous; but we cannot do more than catalogue the principal amongst them, giving their names, as far as possible, in chronological order. **J. G. Albrechtsberger** (1736—1809) is chiefly known to us through the medium of his elaborate work on harmony, counterpoint, and composition; but he wrote as many as twenty-six masses, and numerous other smaller works, chiefly ecclesiastical. **Michael Haydn** (1737—1806), a younger brother of the great Haydn, was greatly esteemed by the latter for his sacred compositions, which included masses, motets, canticles, and other liturgical music. **C. D. Dittersdorf** (1739—1799) produced thirty-seven operas, over forty symphonies, and a number of other forgotten works. **J. André** (1741—1799) wrote German operas. **J. G. Naumann** (1741—1801), composer of oratorios, masses, operas, and symphonies, still survives in occasional ex-

tracts from his larger works. **J. P. Martini** (1741—1816) wrote masses, a *Requiem*, and several French operas. **J. P. Schulz** (1747—1800) and **Ch. Neefe** (1748—1798)— the latter a master of Beethoven—were both writers of opera. The Abbés **Stadler** (1748—1833) and **Vogler** (1749—1814) were composers principally of Church music : Vogler, however, wrote five operas, and, moreover, was the author of several treatises on the theory of music. **J. P. Reichardt** (1752—1817) wrote thirty operas and some oratorios. **J. Pleyel** (1757—1831) is a familiar name with the pianoforte student. Besides his sonatas and other pianoforte compositions, he wrote a number of larger instrumental works, including symphonies and quartets. **J. L. Dussek** (1761—1812) takes a still higher position in the classical pianoforte school. His sonatas, occasionally heard in the concert-rooms of the present day, abound in originality and artistic power. **D. Steibelt** (1764—1823) was another prolific composer for the pianoforte, and among his works are to be found many excellent studies. **C. F. Zelter** (1758—1832) wrote part-songs and other vocal compositions, and organized the *Liedertafel*, a choir of male voices, said to be the first society of the kind formed in Germany. **Andreas Romberg** (1767—1821) is best known in this country in connection with the popular *Lay of the Bell*, a favourite work with local choral societies. He wrote seven operas and several symphonies. Other German composers and teachers of the same period are : Schobert, J. H. Knecht, D. G. Türk, Peter von Winter, J. Preindl, . J. Weigl, B. A. Weber, Wenzel Müller, and B. Romberg, brother of the Andreas Romberg mentioned above.

50. (I.) The leading Italian composers of the latter half of the 18th and the commencement of the 19th centuries were not so numerous as those of Germany. **L. Boccherini** (1740—1806) stands almost alone in the domain of purely orchestral music. **G. B.**

Viotti (1753—1824), the celebrated violinist, and founder of a new school of violin-playing, wrote a number of concertos, chiefly for his own instrument, and with an especial view to the display of his own marvellous powers of execution. The only notable composer of pianoforte music was **Muzio Clementi** (1752—1832), whose *Gradus ad Parnassum* and twelve *Sonatinas* are likely to remain familiar subjects of study for years to come. Clementi was a prince among teachers, and during his lengthy stay in England exercised a remarkable influence upon the art of pianoforte-playing in this country. His grave lies within the precincts of Westminster Abbey, and a small tablet marks the spot. **A. Salieri** (1750—1825), **N. Zingarelli** (1752—1837), **D. Cimarosa** (1754—1801), **S. Mayer** (1763—1845), and **F. Paer** (1771—1839), were all composers of oratorios, masses, or operas, but their works are now nearly forgotten, save by a few musical antiquaries.

51. (F.) **M. L. Cherubini** (1760—1842) was a native of Florence, but having at the age of 26 settled in Paris, where he took up his permanent abode, he is properly classed by some historians as belonging rather to France than to Italy. A pupil of Sarti, an able teacher of that time, Cherubini made rapid progress in the art, and at the age of 22 produced his first opera, *Il Quinto Fabio*. To the Paris public he introduced himself by *Demophon*, but this work failed to command a positive success. In 1791, however, he completely won the popular favour by the production of *Lodoiska*. Undoubtedly his best opera is *Les Deux Journées*, which he brought out in the year 1800; this work is not unknown to the stage of the present day. Other operas were *Medea, Eliza, Anacréon, Faniska, Les Abencérages,* and *Ali Baba*. But Cherubini's fame rests not so much on his work for the stage as that for the Church. His masses, notably the one in D minor, are grand and impressive compositions, and for their

scholarly treatment alone are worthy of especial study.
The same may be said of the *Requiem* in C minor,
written in 1810.   In 1835, Cherubini wrote a *Requiem*
for male voices only, for the commemorative service in
honour of BOIELDIEU (1775—1834), one of his own
pupils, himself a popular writer of opera.   Cherubini's
well-known treatise on Counterpoint, Canon, and Fugue
establishes his position as a master in the art.   The
work was written in the French language, and has been
translated into English by Mr. Cowden Clarke.   As a
composer, Cherubini was highly esteemed by Beethoven,
who pronounced him "the most estimable of living
musicians."   An important contemporary of Cherubini
was **E. H. Mehul** (1763—1817), whose operas were at
one time very popular.   The principal of these were
Joseph, Euphrosyne, Stratonice, and *L'Irato.*   Excerpts
from *Joseph* are still occasionally published in France
and England, but the work is not now performed, except
in Germany.   A single overture (*Le Jeune Henri*)
seems to be the only composition by Mehul which has
really survived this once popular composer.   Among
other French contemporaries of Cherubini we may note
J. F. LESUEUR (1764—1837), O. F. LANGLÉ (1741—
1807), and PIERRE RODE (1774—1830).

52. (G.) LUDWIG VAN BEETHOVEN, the greatest among
German composers, and the most universal musical
genius the world has ever produced, was born at Bonn,
1770, and was the son of a tenor in the Electoral
chapel.   The father, a man given to intemperate habits,
was, while he lived, a source of misery to his son, as
well as to the whole family, who were kept in a state of
poverty approaching to destitution.   Ludwig, who
showed early signs of musical talent, was regarded by
his father as a possible source of enrichment, and on
this account was forced to practise upon the pianoforte
so many hours at a stretch that his studies became a
positive slavery to him.   He received his first lessons
from Van den Eeden, the Court organist, but the suc-

ceeding organist, Neefe, gave him more methodical instruction. Such was the progress he made, that at the age of 12 he occasionally took Neefe's place at the chapel organ; and at the age of 13 (1783) was entrusted with the post of cembalist (pianist)—then an important position, in the orchestra attached to the Court Theatre. His great ambition, however, was to go to Vienna for the completion of his studies, and in 1785 he was enabled to carry out this project. Arrived in Vienna he sought out Mozart, who at first, it is said, received him somewhat coldly, but on hearing him play an improvisation on a given theme, was so astounded that he said to his friends, "Pay heed to this youth; he will one day astonish the world." The opinion of Mozart, then in the zenith of his popularity, did not, however, have an immediate effect on the fortunes of the young musician. Beethoven had already published (1783), when in his 13th year, some small compositions, including three sonatas, which were dedicated to the Elector of Cologne, his patron at Bonn. During this first sojourn in Vienna, which lasted about two years, he appears to have given himself up entirely to study. In 1787 he was recalled to Bonn, by the death of his mother, his affection for whom was heightened by the fact that she was as affectionate and watchful as his father was harsh and neglectful. He had now virtually to provide for the maintenance of his family, and was obliged to have recourse to teaching, an occupation which he always disliked. The only bright spot in his life at this period was the intimate and lasting friendship he formed with the Breuning family— Madame Breuning (a widow), her three sons, and a daughter. In their society Beethoven spent many happy hours of relaxation, and in their company made his acquaintance with the classic literature of the world, and especially of his own language. Here, too (at Bonn), he gained the friendship and assistance of the Count Waldstein, to whom he dedicated the well-known

sonata which is now identified with the Count's name.
To the influence of Waldstein is attributed the appointment of Beethoven, about this time, as Court pianist.
In 1792, having been granted a pension by the Elector,
Beethoven was enabled to revisit Vienna, and so left
Bonn, never to return. Again settled at Vienna, and
this time under more favourable circumstances, Beethoven placed himself under the tuition of Haydn.
But, unhappily, there was no real friendship between
them. Men of temperaments more opposite in character it would be hard to conceive : Haydn was mild and
equable, Beethoven was enthusiastic and eccentric.
Beethoven thought he had reason to complain of the
indifference and actual negligence of his master, but
notwithstanding these misgivings, he continued to re-
ceive lessons from Haydn until 1784, when the latter
left Vienna on a visit to London. Beethoven availed
himself of this departure to attach himself to Albrechtsberger, then organist of the cathedral, under whom he
remained about fifteen months, and with whom he got
on little better than with Haydn. Nevertheless, there
is ample evidence that he worked unceasingly all this
time. (The result of his studies is supposed to be
shown in the work entitled *Studien im Generalbass,*
published under Beethoven's name, but it has been
pretty clearly proved that only a small proportion of
this book is Beethoven's sole and actual work.) It
was in the year 1795 that Beethoven commenced his
public career as a composer and performer. At the
annual concert, for this year, in aid of the widows and
orphans of musicians, Beethoven produced the pianoforte concerto in C major, himself being the pianist.
This performance was a sudden revelation to the Vien-
nese public, and from this time engagements crowded
upon him. During the seven years that followed, he published the thirty-two sonatas, three concertos, two symphonies, nine trios, and numerous other smaller works.
But in 1800 the greatest calamity that could befall a

musician overtook Beethoven—deafness. It is remarkable that nearly all, if not all, his nine symphonies were composed under this affliction. The following are their dates : *First Symphony*, in C major, 1800 ; Second, in D major, dedicated to his patron, Prince Lichnowsky, 1802 ; Third (the *Eroica*), 1803—4 ; Fourth, in B flat major, 1806 ; Fifth, in C minor, about 1808 ; Sixth (*Pastorale*), in F major, about 1808 ; Seventh, in A major, 1812 ; Eighth, in F major, 1812 ; Ninth (the great *Choral Symphony*), in D minor, 1822—3. The only opera Beethoven wrote was *Leonora*, produced in 1805, and condemned by the critics. He wrote new overtures, making four in all, to the work ; and under the new title of *Fidelio*, it was once more presented. This was in the year 1814. In Church music Beethoven was not prolific. His first Mass, in C major, composed in 1807 ; the *Missa Solemnis*, in D major, 1818—22; *The Mount of Olives*, a short oratorio (in which occurs the well-known *Hallelujah*), about 1800 ; appear to be his only sacred compositions. His works have been thus roughly summarized by Czerny :—One opera, two dramas with music, a melodrama, several single dramatic choruses and songs, one oratorio, two masses, nine symphonies, eleven overtures, one septet, seven pianoforte concertos, one violin concerto, two violin quintets, seventeen violin quartets, five violin trios, thirty-five solo sonatas for pianoforte, ten sonatas for pianoforte and violin, six sonatas for pianoforte and violoncello, seven trios for pianoforte, violin, and violoncello, a pianoforte quintet, a great many other pianoforte compositions, cantatas, songs with pianoforte accompaniments, &c. As a *virtuoso* on the pianoforte, Beethoven out-distanced all his rivals, including the celebrated Hummel, who was studying under Mozart at the period of Beethoven's first visit to Vienna. Beethoven owed much of his command of orchestral resources to his practical acquaintance with the stringed instruments, any of which he was able to play, and to this cause in a special degree the beauty and finish of his string trios, quartets, and quintets, are due. It has been asserted that Beethoven's horn parts are often weak; some saying that his want of familiarity with that instrument made him timid in its employment; others, that he was apt to give it impossible passages. To both these accusations the horn part in the *Septet* alone ought to be a sufficient answer, and the *Septet* was a comparatively early production (1800). Notwithstanding incessant hard work, and a career of almost uninterrupted artistic triumph, Beethoven's last years were haunted by a dread of approaching poverty, for which, however, there was no real cause. He died at Vienna (1827), and was publicly buried with great pomp.

53. (G.) **J. N. Hummel** (1778—1837) received his early lessons from Mozart, and even while a boy is said to have been a wonderful performer on the pianoforte. In after years he was considered a worthy rival of Beethoven in the art of extemporization. He principally devoted himself to the pianoforte, both as player and composer. Schlüter says of him: "After the three great masters, Hummel is the best pianoforte (not sonata) composer; and, as such, is the founder of a school which has cast into the shade Dussek, Steibelt, Pleyel, Wölfl, and others." In Church music his masses take high rank even now, and the one in B flat is frequently performed. Hummel also very successfully adapted the symphonies of Haydn and Mozart, and some of Beethoven's also, for pianoforte, flute, violin, and violoncello. A *Septet*, written for pianoforte, string and wind instruments, is Hummel's *chef d'œuvre.* His operas—and he wrote several—are now forgotten. S. Neukomm (1778—1858), who wrote in all departments of composition; A. Reicha (1770—1836), author of the well-known work on fugue; A. Diabelli (1781—1858); C. Kreutzer (1782—1849), who composed twenty-four operas and a number of masses, were among the most esteemed German musicians of this time.

54. (G.) **Ludwig Spohr** (1784—1859), a native of
Brunswick, developed at a very early age that remarkable talent for the violin which placed him amongst the
most brilliant violinists of his time. At the age of 14
he obtained the patronage of the Duke of Brunswick,
who placed him in his orchestra, and subsequently em
ployed Franz Eck, an excellent player, to give him
lessons. Of his long and successful career as a performer we shall not now speak : the D minor and E
minor concertos, both composed at an early period,
bear sufficient testimony to his executive powers, as
well as to his skill as a composer of violin music. As
a writer, with the exception of a few lessons received
in his youth, it is said that Spohr was entirely self-
taught. This accounts for much of the freedom, some
would say lawlessness, which characterizes all Spohr's
work. His first opera, *Alruna*, had a considerable
local success, but it is now entirely forgotten. However, the reception accorded to this work encouraged
·Spohr to further efforts in opera, and in 1816 *Faust*
was produced at Prague. Spohr's *Faust*, since eclipsed
by Gounod's immortal work, contains many fine points,
and should not have been allowed to fall into unmerited
neglect. Seven years later *Jessonda* was produced at
the Court Theatre of Cassel, to which Spohr had been
appointed as director. These are his two great operas ;
Zemire und Azor had but a fleeting popularity, and
other operas were even more short-lived. Of his oratorios, *The Last Judgment* is the best known in this
country ; *Calvary* (1835) deserves a more frequent
hearing. In 1820 Spohr came over to England to con-
duct one of the Philharmonic Concerts, and under his
own bâton was produced, for the first time and in
manuscript, the *Symphony in D minor*. The symphony
entitled *Die Weihe der Töne* (The Consecration of Sound),
an ever-present feature in our orchestral programmes, was
produced in 1832. *The Fall of Babylon* was composed
for and produced at the Norwich Musical Festival of

1842 ; in 1843 Spohr himself conducted a performance of the work at Exeter Hall, by the Sacred Harmonic Society. Besides the works already mentioned, Spohr composed eight symphonies, including the *Historical* and the *Seasons*, a double quartet for strings, and a number of works in which the violin figures as the principal instrument. As an example of his skill in part writing may be mentioned his Mass for ten voices, composed for the Leipsic Choral Society, but relinquished by that body as impracticable. Spohr, however, successfully produced it at Cassel, in 1827. Spohr's choral music, although highly esteemed amongst us, is yet so difficult by reason of the "chromatic" progressions in which he freely indulges, that few vocal societies find the courage to attempt it in public. His instrumental works are in constant use and request, while his two great violin concertos are frequently selected by modern *virtuosi* as admirable vehicles for the display of their skill on the most difficult of all instruments.

55. (G.) **Karl Maria von Weber** (1786—1826), the son of a travelling actor—once a man of wealth and good social position—had the good fortune to be placed under the tuition of Michael Haydn (par. 49). Of his juvenile productions—including two comic operas—it is needless to speak : Weber's actual career as a composer did not commence until he had visited Vienna (in 1803), where he studied for some months under the Abbé Vogler (par. 49). The following year Weber was appointed to the directorship of the opera-house at Breslau. Here he had a narrow escape of being accidentally poisoned. A succession of worldly reverses subsequently induced him to accept the post of private secretary to Prince Ludwig of Wurtemberg. In the year 1811 he obtained the countenance of the Grand Duke of Wurtemberg to a new opera, *Abu Hassan*, the success of which enabled Weber to make a professional tour amongst the principal cities of Germany. In 1813

he obtained the appointment—a comparatively important one—of musical director of the theatre at Prague; for which he composed several new works. Thence he removed to Dresden (1816) in the capacity of Kapell Meister to the King of Saxony. We cannot stay to enumerate the many compositions (among them the *Jubilee Cantata* and the Mass in E flat) which emanated from Weber's pen at this period. A new, and the most brilliant, era of his life was commenced with the opera *Der Freischütz*, originally intended for the Berlin Theatre. The same year, 1820, he completed *Preciosa*, and this work was produced before its predecessor. The success of *Preciosa*, marked as it was, was as nothing compared with that of *Der Freischütz*, the fame of which quickly spread to this country, and occasioned an invitation of the composer to London, as well as the commission to write *Oberon* for the English stage. In 1823 *Euryanthe* was produced, at Vienna, but the success of the opera was very transient, and gave Weber considerable disappointment. Acting on the advice of Beethoven, Weber subsequently curtailed the work, and thus obtained for it a wider hearing. Weber paid his promised visit to London in the year 1826, bringing with him his opera *Oberon*, which was produced at Covent Garden under his own bâton. An internal disorder of long standing, aggravated no doubt by hard work and continuous anxiety, prematurely terminated his life. He died suddenly, at the close of his engagement at Covent Garden, and was buried in London. Some years afterwards his remains were removed to Germany, and were re-interred at Dresden. The great work of Weber's life was the development of a distinct school of German opera. His *Der Freischütz* and *Euryanthe* must always be regarded—the period of their production duly considered—as among the most important contributions to the rising school. Schlüter regards Wagner's *Lohengrin* as the offspring of *Euryanthe* by "direct descent." *Euryanthe*, however, has

long been shelved, owing, no doubt, to the weakness of
its libretto ; but *Der Freischütz* enjoys an undiminished
popularity.   It is affirmed by some that it was Weber
who originated the plan of including in the opera
overture the leading airs from the body of the work.
It is, however, to be noticed that the same feature exists
in the overture to *Don Giovanni* (1787), a work which
dates many years before Weber's operas.

56. (G.) **Franz Schubert** (1797—1828) began his
career as a chorister in the Imperial Chapel at Vienna,
where he remained until his 16th year.   Of his
juvenile efforts at this period we shall not speak ; we
should, however, make an exception of the celebrated
song *Hagar's Lament*, which shows how early his wonderful powers as a song-composer were developed.
When the loss of his treble voice brought an end to
his chorister's duties, he returned to his native town in
the capacity of schoolmaster's assistant in his father's
school.   Here he composed a number of works, including the *Mass in F*, which, slight as it is in construction,
is a charming composition ; and well deserves the in-
creased attention which has of late years been accorded
to it in this country.   The Masses in C and G were
composed about 1815 ; the same year were produced an
enormous number of songs, including *The Erl King*,
highly prized by Goethe.   At the age of 20 Schubert
left his home to reside in Vienna, and subsequently
entered the service of Count Esterhazy as music-master
to his children, where he remained about two years.
After this Schubert never held any definite appointment, but lived an erratic kind of life, although he was
seldom out of Vienna.   He once applied for a post in
the Imperial Chapel, but failed.   He formed but few
permanent friendships, and did not succeed in winning
the regard of Beethoven until the latter was on his
death-bed.   As a composer for the opera, Schubert was
exceedingly active and uniformly unsuccessful.   The

music to *Rosamunde*, originally produced at the "An der Wien" Theatre, in 1823, appears to be the best example of his efforts in this class of composition. A few years ago the music of *Rosamunde* was brought before a London audience at the Crystal Palace, Sydenham, but we do not know of any further attempt to keep it alive. Next to his marvellous songs, Schubert's pianoforte works are the most popular amongst his compositions. His sonatas are, as a rule, somewhat erratic in point of musical form, but they are all full of strong connected interest, and exhibit in a remarkable degree the inexhaustible fertility of Schubert's mind. The same may be said of the pianoforte *fantasies*. In the domain of chamber music, his most important composition is, perhaps, the octet for stringed and wind instruments, occasionally performed in this country. Of Schubert's nine symphonies undoubtedly the finest is the symphony in C, composed in 1828, the year of his death. The score of his unfinished symphony in B minor presents so many characteristic beauties that it is a matter for regret that he did not complete the work. Of his Church music, to the works already mentioned must be added the *Mass in E flat* (composed in 1828), which is frequently performed in this country. Schubert also wrote several cantatas—including *Miriam's Battle Song*—melodramas, marches, and other occasional compositions, but all these save the marches are now nearly forgotten.

57. (G.) The name of **Jacob Meyerbeer** (1794—1864) is indissolubly associated with French Opera, but he was a German not only by birth but by training, and was a fellow-disciple with Weber under the Abbé Vogler at Vienna, at which city Meyerbeer was known as a brilliant pianist. His early operas—*Jephtha's Daughter* and *The Two Caliphs*, produced in Germany, and *Romilda, Semiramide riconosciuta, Margherita d'Anjou*, and others, for the Italian stage,—were by no means so successful as his later works in Paris. *Robert*

le Diable, produced at the Paris Grand Opera in 1831,
at once established the fame of its composer. *Robert*
was followed by *Les Huguenots* (1836); *L'Etoile du
Nord* (originally in German), 1854; *Le Prophète*
(1849); *Le Pardon de Ploermel*—better known as
Dinorah (1859); and *L'Africaine* (1864). The greater
part of Meyerbeer's life was spent in Paris, and Rossini
was the only composer who rivalled him in popularity.
Among the lesser German contemporaries of Meyerbeer
we should give the first mention to **J. Moscheles**
(1794—1870), so celebrated for his pianoforte playing
that Mendelssohn, who was in a position to command
the best masters, availed himself of Moscheles' tuition.
Moscheles held for some time the position of professor of
the pianoforte at the Leipsic conservatorium. He composed, besides some symphonies, a number of concertos,
sonatas, and variations for his especial instrument, and
his works still occupy occasional places in our concert-
programmes. FERDINAND RIES (1784—1838) was a
pupil of Beethoven, and excelled as a pianist.   He
composed several pianoforte concertos and sonatas; also
two operas, besides quartets and other chamber music.
F. KALKBRENNER (1784—1849) was another accomplished pianoforte player, and has left behind him
many studies which are highly prized by pianoforte
teachers.   With one or two notable exceptions the
names of F. E. FESCA (1789—1826); J. C. F.
SCHNEIDER (1786—1858); P. J. LINDPAINTNER (1791—
1856); J. MAYSEDER (1789—1863); B. KLEIN
(1794—1832); C. CZERNY (1791—1857), whose pianoforte studies are familiar to the students of the present
day; M. HAUPTMANN (1794—1868) well remembered
as the teacher of many living musicians; A. B. MARX
(1799—1866); C. REISSIGER (1789—1859) bring the
catalogue of German composers down to our own day.

58. (G.) FELIX MENDELSSOHN-BARTHOLDY (1809—
1847), born in Hamburg, was the son of a wealthy banker,
who on discovering his child's precocious talent for

music spared no pains in fostering and developing it both by direct tuition of celebrated professors and by the refining influence of the highest musical society. Brought up in an atmosphere of musical culture from infancy, Mendelssohn had opportunities which seldom fall to the lot of a musical student, and availed himself of them to the fullest extent. On the removal of the family to Berlin, Mendelssohn received his pianoforte instruction from Berger, the principal pianist there, and for composition was placed under Zelter, a pupil of Sebastian Bach : this combined course began when Mendelssohn was but eight years old. Under Zelter he continued some years ; but at this time his parents had no thought of his devoting himself entirely to music as a profession. This was not decided until the year 1825, when, on visiting and playing before Cherubini, in Paris, he obtained the enthusiastic approbation of that great master. The first composition of any importance was the *Symphony in C minor*, written in 1824, when Mendelssohn was but 15. In 1825, the opera, *The Wedding of Camacho*, was produced at Berlin, but while it had a hearty reception at the hands of the public, the Berlin press was hostile to the work. Two years afterwards (1827) came the overture to the *Midsummer Night's Dream;* and, in the following year, the descriptive overture *A Calm Sea and Prosperous Voyage.* To about the same period is attributed the *Reformation Symphony,* introduced into England a few years back by Mr. Manns at the Crystal Palace. The year 1829 was marked by Mendelssohn's first visit to England,* he having just completed his studies at the University of Berlin. He appeared at several London concerts, and was warmly received on all sides. A short trip to Scotland occasioned the overture entitled *Fingal's Cave*, or *The Hebrides*, produced on his return

---

* Professor Ritter (History of Music, p. 394) gives 1827 as the date of this visit. The invitation (from Moscheles) came in that year, but the journey was deferred until 1829.

to Berlin, in the same year. In 1830 Mendelssohn
proceeded on a tour through Italy and Switzerland,
and while at Rome composed the music to *The First
Walpurgis Night* of Goethe. In 1833, after having
failed to obtain the principal professorship at the
Berlin *Sing-Academie*, he was appointed "Municipal
Music Director" at Düsseldorf, where he commenced
the oratorio, *St. Paul*. From Düsseldorf he was sum-
moned to the directorship of the Gewandhaus concerts
at Leipsic, and while there completed his *St. Paul*, the
first performance of which took place at the Düsseldorf
festival of 1836. In the autumn of the following year
St. Paul was produced at the Birmingham festival,
under the composer's direction. The public celebration,
at Leipsic, in 1840, of the fourth centenary of the invention of the art of printing, occasioned the production of the *Festgesang* and the *sinfonia cantata, Lobgesang*, (*Hymn of Praise*). The former cantata was
sung in the public square at Leipsic, on the unveiling
of the statue of Guttenberg ; the Hymn of Praise
was performed in St. Thomas's Church. (The recent
Caxton Commemoration Festival, 1877, was similarly
marked by a performance of this work in Westminster
Abbey, under the direction of Dr. Bridge, the organist.)
In 1841 Mendelssohn accepted the appointment of
Kapell-meister to the King of Prussia, for whom he
composed, as his inaugural work, the music to the *Antigone*. The year 1843 witnessed the accomplishment
of a long-cherished project of Mendelssohn's — the
Leipsic Conservatorium of Music—of which he was the
founder and first director. Among the original professors were Schumann and Hauptmann. Mendelssohn's
last great work was the *Elijah*, which was expressly
composed for, and produced at, the Birmingham Festival of 1846. An opera, *Lorelei*, and an oratorio,
Christus, were both left unfinished. His death, in
1847, took place at Leipsic, and his remains were conveyed for interment to Berlin. It is needless to give a

full list of his works, which are well known in this country. The disciples of a new school have protested against the general idolization of Mendelssohn which would place him on a par with Handel and Beethoven; but, in spite of all that can be adduced against him, Mendelssohn continues to maintain a high position in the popular esteem. Rarely, if ever, is any scheme of "Classical Concerts," whether of orchestral or of chamber-music, marked by an utter exclusion of works from the comprehensive repertory which Mendelssohn has left behind him. All his compositions—from his symphonies to the charming *Lieder ohne worte*—from the *Elijah* to the *Anthems for two Choirs*—breathe a life and freshness, a sublimity and devoutness, which more than compensate for an occasional absence of detailed and formal construction.

59. (G.) **Robert Schumann** (1810—1856), a native of Zwickau, Saxony, was educated at Leipsic for the legal profession, but eventually abandoned his studies in favour of music. Under the care of WIECK his remarkable powers as a pianist were rapidly developed, while his theory studies were directed by Heinrich Dorn. In the year 1834 Schumann brought out the *Neue Zeitschrift für Musik*, a journal which still exists, and in it he published a number of essays and sketches on musical subjects—all full of literary power and keen critical perception. So far, Schumann had confined himself principally to compositions for the pianoforte, among which we should mention the *Sonata in F sharp minor*, that in G minor, and the *Fantasias;* and it was not until 1841 that he attempted his first symphony, in B flat. In 1843, the Cantata, *Paradise and the Peri,* a setting of the story from Moore's *Lalla Rookh,* was produced at Leipsic, but did not create any very decided impression. An opera, *Geneviève,* produced in 1848, also proved unsuccessful. The same year the music to *Manfred,* excerpts from which are occasionally performed in this country, was written. Schumann's finest work

of this class, however, is his music to *Faust*, a work full
of beauty and power, which deserves to be better known
and more widely appreciated. This was produced in
1850. In the same year Schumann was appointed
to the Directorship of Music at Düsseldorf, but his
confirmed ill-health, and the increasing symptoms of
mental disorder, prevented him from undertaking much
active duty, although as a writer he was still very prolific, producing his *Symphony in E flat* (1851), and
several fine works, including *The Minstrel's Curse,
Hermann and Dorothea*, and *The Pilgrimage of the
Rose*. But, in 1854, insanity took complete possession
of him, and after an ineffectual attempt to drown himself in the Rhine, he was conveyed to a private asylum
in the neighbourhood of Bonn, where, in 1856, he
died. The claims of Schumann as a composer were
almost unknown in this country until his widow, the
gifted pianist Clara Schumann, by her wonderful playing of his works for the pianoforte, brought to light
her husband's exalted genius, which was too far in
advance of his own time to obtain the immediate recog-
nition which his illustrious contemporary, Mendelssohn,
received.

60. **Frederic Chopin** (1810—1849), a native of
Warsaw, spent by far the greater portion of his artistic
life in Paris, and his works are strongly tinctured with
the style of the French School. His dance-music,
especially his *Polonaises*, based on the form of an old .
national dance in Poland, is remarkable for the under-
lying melancholy which in fact more or less characterizes all Chopin's works. His *Mazourkas, Studies,
Nocturnes, Waltzes, Galops*, and *Impromptus*, as well
as the *Polonaises*, are all familiar compositions in the
drawing-room, as well as in our concert-rooms. Chopin
introduced several new features in pianoforte scoring.
"It is to him," says Liszt in his well-known *Life of
Chopin*, "that we owe the extension of chords, struck
together in arpeggio, or *en batterie*; in the chromatic

sinuosities of which his pages offer such striking examples; the little groups of superadded notes falling like light drops of pearly dew upon the melodic figure." His sonatas, the first of which contains *The Funeral March*, and his concertos serve to exhibit every variety of sentiment and passion, in which, however, pathos strongly predominates. Chopin died of decline at an early age (39), and the March to which we have alluded was performed at his funeral.

61. (**F.**) The list of celebrated French composers of the period succeeding our last summary of this school is a brief one. **Daniel Auber** (1782*—1871) for many years director of the Paris Conservatoire, devoted himself principally to opera. His best known works are *Fra Diavolo, ·Le Domino Noir*, and *Masaniello* (*La Muette de Portici*). L. HEROLD (1791—1833) lives through his famous opera, *Zampa* (1830); other operas were *Marie* and *Le Pré aux Clercs*. **Hector Berlioz** (1803—1869), whose intimate acquaintance with every possible resource of the orchestra led him into the composition of works which require the employment of large and abnormally constituted bands to produce them, was originally a medical student, but afterwards went through the music course at the Conservatoire of Paris. He produced a large number of works, chiefly orchestral, of which his symphonies, *Episode de la vie d'un artiste, Harold en Italie, Romeo et Juliette*, and the *Fantastique*, are the principal. His opera *Benvenuto Cellini* is still, we believe, occasionally performed in France. HALEVY (1799—1862), besides his greatest opera, *La Juive*, so popular in Paris, wrote several operas, among them *L'Eclair*, and *Les Mousquetaires de la Reine*. FÉLICIEN DAVID (1810—1876), whose symphony-ode, *The Desert*, was revived, after long neglect, at Paris shortly after his death, brings us to the end of the list of completed careers.

---

* Schlüter and some others mention 1784 as the date of Auber's birth.

62. (I.) **G. Spontini** (1784—1851) effected considera-
ble improvements on the style of Gluck, to whom also
he, more nearly than any other composer, approaches in
classic dignity.   Like Gluck, Spontini, after a brief
Italian career, settled in Paris (1803), and for the Paris
Opera wrote his master-piece, *La Vestale*, as well as the
operas, *Ferdinand, Cortez,* and *Olympie.*   Professor
Ritter, who, as we think, mistakenly fixes the date of
Spontini's birth ten years earlier, thus writes of him :
" Animated by a sense of heroic grandeur, full of pathos
and passionate expression, he necessarily gave to his
forms an adequate amplitude and vigour of style.   But
not this quality alone characterizes his works : tender-
ness of feeling, and sympathy for the softer chords of
human passion, are also familiar to his pen.   Amidst
all the brilliancy of scenic representations, he seldom
becomes trivial, or degenerates into mere superficial
effect.   His effects are always sustained by noble
dramatic meaning.   His orchestral accompaniments
and illustrations are vigorous, sonorous, and brilliant,
according to the requirements of the scenic situation."
All this is amply proved on a mere glance at the score
of his *Vestale,* which ought to find an English publisher,
and a place in every musician's library.

63. (I.) **Gioachino Rossini** (1792—1868), a native
of Pezaro, in Italy, early distinguished himself at the
school of music at Bologna, where he studied composition under Johann Martini.   While yet a boy, he wrote
several operas for the provincial theatres, and at the
age of 21 produced *Tancredi* at Venice.   In 1816
Rossini went to Rome, and produced, at the Carnival
of that year, the *Barbiere di Siviglia* and another opera.
Otello was performed at Naples shortly afterwards, and
at Rome *La Cenerentola,* while at Milan *La Guzza
Ladra* found immediate favour.   All these works were
written in the same year—1816.   *Mosè in Egitto* (in
which the celebrated prayer, *To Thee, great Lord—Dal
tuo stellato Soglio*—was inserted as an afterthought), was

produced in 1818, and *La Donna del Lago* in the year following. In 1823 took place the first performance of *Semiramide*, at Venice. After a short and successful visit to London, Rossini went to Paris, where he remained for the rest of his life. The only opera of note composed for the Parisians was the fine work *Guglielmo Tell*, which appeared in 1829. After this date no other compositions, except the *Stabat Mater* and the posthumous *Messe Solennelle*, appeared from his pen. The most prominent among Rossini's Italian contemporaries were : **V. Bellini** (1802—1835), whose *Norma, La Sonnambula*, and *I Puritani*, are his only lasting operas ; **G. Donizetti** (1797—1848), the composer of *Lucrezia Borgia, Lucia di Lammermoor, La Favorita, Don Pasquale, L'Elisire d'Amore, La Fille du Regiment*, and other favourite operas; S. MERCADANTE (1797 — 1870), and M. CARAFA (1785 — 1872) both truthfully described as " weak imitators of Rossini."

64. (E.) **Samuel Wesley** (1766—1837) was a son of the Rev. Charles Wesley, the great hymn-writer. Samuel Wesley is said to have attempted composition even in childhood; at the age of six years he wrote an oratorio, *Ruth*—a mere childish production, as might have been expected, but still showing signs of unusual musical taste and ability. Wesley's anthems are among the finest of his time. They must not, however, be confounded with those of **Samuel Sebastian Wesley** (1810—1876), his son, whose *Blessed be the God and Father*, and *The Wilderness*, and other anthems and Church Music, stamp him as one of the greatest Church writers of the age. **William Crotch** (1775—1847) was another in whom genius was early discovered and developed. He has left behind him the oratorios, *The Captivity*, and *Palestine*, and a number of anthems, services, glees, and a work on Harmony. His grand motett, *Methinks I hear the full Celestial Choir*, is frequently performed, and may be cited as an exquisite specimen of vocal writing in five parts. For

some years Dr. Crotch filled the Chair of Music at the University of Oxford. **Thomas Attwood** (1767—1838) was a pupil of Mozart, under whose careful training he acquired that sweetness of style and clearness of diction for which his writings are noted.   He composed a number of anthems—of which *Come, Holy Ghost* is the most popular—and several operas, now unknown. **J. B. Cramer** (1771—1858) was a leading pianist and teacher, and composed upwards of 100 pianoforte sonatas, seven concertos, numerous studies, and the well-known instruction book.   **John Field** (1782—1837), a pupil of Clementi, was another accomplished pianoforte player and composer, whose *nocturnes* are ever favourite compositions. **Sir H. R. Bishop** (1782—1855) was a prolific composer of almost every kind of music, but excelled in the part-song and glee.   He wrote many popular operas in English, and from these many of his best-known songs and choruses are taken. **V. Wallace** (1814—1865) survives in his operas, *Maritana, Lurline,* &c.   **M. W. Balfe** (1808—1870), an Irishman by birth, but an Italian by training, composed principally for the stage.   His operas, *The Bohemian Girl,* and *The Talisman,* a posthumous work, are at the present moment the most prominent of Balfe's productions.   **Sir William Sterndale Bennett** (1816—1875), one of the most gifted of English composers, was not a prolific writer, but everything he has left us is of the highest merit.   His two cantatas, *The May-Queen* and *The Woman of Samaria,* are beautiful works of their kind.   Of his orchestral works, the *Symphony in G minor,* the concert overtures, *The Wood Nymph, Paradise and the Peri,* and the pianoforte concertos, are among the best. **Cipriani Potter,** a former principal of the Royal Academy of Music, is still remembered as a skilful teacher and an accomplished writer.

65. (**E.**) The more prominent among the composers of our own day shall now be briefly noticed.   **Sir John Goss** (*b.* 1800), sometime organist of St. Paul's Cathe-

dral, was in boyhood a chorister of the Chapel Royal,
and afterwards became a pupil of Attwood, at St. Paul's.
He has composed a large number of works, chiefly
sacred. Among his anthems the best known are, *If we
believe that Jesus died* (composed for the funeral of the
Duke of Wellington), *Praise the Lord, O give thanks,
O Saviour of the World, Stand up and bless the Lord
your God,* and *O taste and see how gracious the Lord
is.* His secular works include *Ossian's Hymn to the
Sun, There is beauty on the Mountain, The Sycamore
Shade, &c.* Sir John Goss was formerly a Professor in
the Royal Academy of Music, and his work on *Harmony and Thorough-bass* is a well-known and widely
popular text-book. **Sir Julius Benedict** (*b.* 1804),
composer of *The Lily of Killarney* and other operas,
and of the oratorio, *St. Peter,* is a native of Stuttgart,
Germany, but has been resident in England for
many years. **Sir Michael Costa** (*b.* 1810) composer of the popular oratorio, *Eli,* and of *Naaman,*
has also written several operas, among which may be
mentioned *Malvina* and *Don Carlos.* He is the conductor of Her Majesty's Opera, and of the Sacred Harmonic Society. **G. A. Macfarren** (*b.* 1813), Professor
of Music in the University of Cambridge, and Principal
of the Royal Academy of Music, has written an immense
number of works, chiefly vocal, among them the two
oratorios, *St. John the Baptist* and *The Resurrection.*
Edward J. Hopkins (*b.* 1818), organist of the Temple
Church, London, ranks with the best Church writers of
the present day. His *Services* in F and A, his anthems
and hymn-tunes, are deservedly esteemed, and will have
a permanent place in the music-literature of the Church.
The **Rev. Sir F. A. Gore Ouseley, Bart**. (*b.* 1825), Professor of Music in the University of Oxford, is the
composer of the oratorios *St. Polycarp* and *Hagar,*
and of several fine anthems, of which *It came even to
pass* is perhaps one of the best. Sir Frederick Ouseley
has written treatises on *Harmony,* on *Counterpoint,*

Canon, and Fugue, and on *Musical Form.* Other
eminent English musicians are : **Sir R. P. Stewart,**
Professor of Music in the University of Dublin, composer of Church music, cantatas, and instrumental
works ; **Dr. Steggall,** organist of Lincoln's Inn, whose
anthems and services are justly esteemed as among the
best of the day ; **F. H. Cowen,** composer of the *Rose
Maiden,* the *Corsair,* dramatic cantatas ; also of *Pauline,*
an opera, and *The Deluge,* an oratorio ; **A. Sullivan,**
composer of *The Prodigal Son, The Light of the
World,* &c. ; **Berthold Tours,** who has written some
fine anthems and Church Services, besides numerous
songs ; **Joseph Barnby,** author of many popular anthems
and services ; **John Barnett,** whose *Mountain Sylph*
is a favourite composition ; **J. F. Barnett,** composer of
The Ancient Mariner, &c. ; **J. L. Hatton,** author of
Hezekiah, (an oratorio), and several anthems, songs, and
part-songs, &c., &c.

66. (F.) CHARLES GOUNOD (*b.* 1818) stands at the
head of French composers at the present day. He has
written some fine sacred works (*Messe Solennelle, Messe
du Sacré Cœur,* &c.), but his fame will rest chiefly upon
his operas, of which *Faust* is his *chef d'œuvre.* Amongst
other leading French composers are **Ambroise Thomas,**
director of the Paris Conservatoire, author of *Mignon,
Hamlet,* and other operas ; **Flotow** (author of *Marta*) ;
Jacques Offenbach, composer of many comic operas,
including *La Grande Duchesse, Barbe Bleu,* &c. ; and
HERVÉ, another writer of *Opera Comique,* whose
Chilperic has had a world-wide but ephemeral popularity. Among other living French musicians may be
mentioned MASSÉ, MASSENET, C. SAINT-SAËNS, LECOCQ,
and GUILMANT.

67. (I.) GIUSEPPE VERDI (*b.* 1814) now stands almost without a contemporary of any importance among
Italians His operas are very numerous, the most
popular among them being *Ernani, Rigoletto, Il Trova-*

tore, La Traviata, Un Ballo in Maschera, and *Aïda.*
His *Requiem,* notwithstanding a frequent disregard of
many important canons of contrapuntal writing, is a
grand and impressive work.

68. **Niels W. Gade** (*b.* 1817), a native of Copenhagen,
one of the most distinguished of living composers, is
chiefly known through his *Erlking's Daughter* and
other cantatas, but he has also written some splendid
symphonies and other orchestral works, as well as
chamber-music and songs. **Anton Rubinstein,** a
native of Russia, better known as a pianist of the first
rank, has also written concertos and other orchestral
pieces, of which latter his recent *Ocean Symphony* is
the most remarkable.

69. **(G.) Richard Wagner** (*b.* 1813), whose art-
theories have for many years been the subject of a great
deal of bitter controversy amongst musicians, has endeavoured to revolutionize the whole system of opera,
and to overturn all previous notions of musical form.
His earlier operas, *Rienzi,* and *Das Liebesverbot,* are
framed upon the old models; but he forsook these in
his *Fliegende Holländer* and *Tannhäuser,* and even these
he considers as far beneath the ideal form of opera.
Lohengrin may be regarded as a more decided advance
upon *Tannhäuser ;* but *Tristan and Isolde* and the
Meistersinger are the first works which embody the full
realization of Wagner's views. His greatest contribution
to the " music of the future " is the well-known opera-
series, *Der Ring der Nibelungen.* This fourfold work
consists of *Das Rheingold, Die Walküre, Siegfried,*
and *Götterdämmerung,* and the whole series was performed at a great public festival, in 1876, at Bayreuth,
Germany, in a theatre especially constructed for that
purpose. A selection from this tetralogy was performed in London, at the Royal Albert Hall, 1877,
under the composer's personal direction. **Franz Liszt**
(*b.* 1811), a native of Hungary, is one of the greatest

of living *virtuosi* on the pianoforte, for which he has
written concertos, and numberless smaller studies and
transcriptions, besides cantatas and symphonies.   Liszt
is a strong advocate of the Wagner theories, to which
we shall refer more particularly in a later section of this
work. **Johannes Brahms** (*b.* 1833), whose *Song of
Destiny* and *Requiem* are becoming familiar works in
this country, has also proved his remarkable genius in
the symphony and other important forms of composition. **J. Raff**, J. Joachim (*b.* 1831), Ernst Pauer, are
all distinguished composers, amongst many others, in
their respective styles.

70. We have now come to the conclusion of our
general summary, which from the nature of our
subject can be little more than biographical.   Our succeeding section will consist of a series of tables of
musicians and events; after which we shall proceed to
trace, with the help afforded by the present section, the
history of the art itself.

SECTION II. — CHRONOMETRICAL TABLES OF MUSICIANS AND MUSICAL EVENTS.

EXPLANATION.

1. EACH page contains a "square," divided into *ten* parts. The squares on opposite pages are duplicates, *i.e.* they represent the same period of time ; the *left* hand page indicating events, discoveries, &c., the *right* hand page containing the names of musicians. From the time of Alfred the Great (870) and onward, the reigns of the English Sovereigns are given in the respective intervals of their accession, in order the more clearly to localize the musical events in the mind of the student.

2. The *first* square (right and left) includes the dates A.D. to A.D. 999. Each succeeding square represents 100 years.

3. Table No. I. contains *ten* spaces of 100 years each ; these again are subdivided into *ten* spaces of *ten* years each. Table No. II. (and each succeeding table) contains *ten* spaces of *ten* years each, each space of ten years being afterwards subdivided into *ten* spaces of *one* year each. These spaces are so arranged that each terminal number of a date has a fixed position in the squares : thus, the date "*xxx*0" is always assigned to the "band" at the top of the square ; the date "*xxx*5" is always to be found in the centre square, and so on.

4. The sign * prefixed to a name or event denotes that the date is uncertain or approximate.

5. It will be well for the student to exercise himself in the identification of dates and squares, by the use of the figures, 0, 1, 2, 3, 4, 5, 6, 7, 8, 9, before systematically employing the tables in conjunction with the text.

Example. To find the year 1555 :—5 is invariably the *centre* figure. Turning to Table VII. (1500—99) we see that 1550 is the *centre* square of ten years, and 1555 the *centre* of that square. A few experiments of this kind will easily familiarize the student with the plan of these tables.

TABLE I.—A.D.   TO 999.

MUSICAL EPOCHS AND EVENTS.

A.D. — to A.D. 99.

100	200	300
.	.	Pope Silvester's Music School in Rome, 330. St. Ambrose arranged Authentic Modes, 390.

400	500	600
.	* Gregory added Plagal Modes, 590—600.	Pope Vitalianus introduces the organ into churches, 657—672.

700	800	900
* Charlemagne spreads Gregory's system through France and Germany, 768—814.	Appearance of troubadours in Provence. Church organs in use.	* Discantus (organum, or *Diaphony*) employed by Hucbald.

TABLE I.—A.D. TO 999.

MUSICIANS.

A.D.

100 — Silvestor. — St. Ambrose d. 397.

200

300

400 — Boethius b.

500 — *Cassiodorus d. — Gregory.

600 — *Isidore d.

700 — Alcuin d. 814. — Alfred I.

800

900 — Athelstan IV. — Edwy. — Edgar. — Edward I. — Edmund I. — Edred. — 5. Edward II. — 8. Ethelrd. II. — Hucbald d.

TABLE II.—A.D. 1000 TO 1099.

MUSICAL EPOCHS AND EVENTS.

1000	
1010	
1020	
1030	Guido, about this period, improves the method of singing, and
1040	* (Guido) names first six notes of scale by letters of alphabet.
1050	
1060	
1070	
1080	
1090	Franco of Cologne assigned this date by Forkel

TABLE II.—A.D. 1000 TO 1099.

MUSICIANS.

1000	1001	1002	1003	1004	1005	1006	1007	1008	1009
1010	1011	1012	1013	1014	1015	1016 *Edmund Canute*	1017	1018	1019
1020	1021	1022	1023	1024	1025	1026	1027	1028	1029
1030	1031	1032	1033	1034	1035	1036	1037	1038	1039
1040 *Hardicanute*	1041	1042 *Edward the Confessor*	1043	1044	1045	1046	1047	1048	1049
1050 *Guido d'Arezzo d.*	1051	1052	1053	1054	1055	1056	1057	1058	1059
1060	1061	1062	1063	1064	1065	1066 *Harold*	1067	1068	1069 *William I.*
1070	1071	1072	1073	1074	1075	1076	1077	1078	1079
1080	1081	1082	1083	1084	1085	1086	1087 *William II.*	1088	1089
1090	1091	1092	1093	1094	1095	1096	1097	1098	1099

N.B.—In the next and following tables, the single years will be denoted by the distinguishing unit figure only.

TABLE III.—A.D. 1100 TO 1199.

MUSICAL EPOCHS AND EVENTS.

1100	1110	1120	1130	1140	1150	1160	1170	1180	1190

Origin and gradual development of present notation.

Church music and Folk songs, with crude harmony.

TABLE III.—A.D. 1100 TO 1199.

MUSICIANS.

TABLE IV.—A.D. 1200 TO 1299.

MUSICAL EPOCHS AND EVENTS.

1200	The Minnesinger in Germany.
1210	
1220	* Franco introduces system of musical measure by shapes of notes.
1230	
1240	Odington (English monk), Treatise on Music.
1250	* Sumer is a cumen in, an English composition, about this date.
1260	Maehron (France), writes on Musical Theory.
1270	
1280	* De la Hale, and other troubadours.
1290	Secular songs in three-part harmony.

TABLE IV.—A.D. 1200 TO 1299.

MUSICIANS.

1200	—1	—2	—3	—4	—5	—6	—7	—8	—9

1210			1220 * Franco of Cologne.			1230		
—11	—12	—13	—1	—2	—3	—1	—2	—3
—14	—15	—16 *Henry III.*	—4	—5	—6	—4	—5	—6
—17	—18	—19	—7	—8	—9	—7	—8	—9
1240 * W. Odington.			1250			1260		
—1	—2	—3	—1	—2	—3	—1	—2	—3
—4	—5	—6	—4	—5	—6	—4	—5	—6
—7	—8	—9	—7	—8	—9	—7	—8	—9
1270			1280			1290 * Adam de la Hale.		
—1	—2 *Edward I.*	—3	—1	—2	—3	—1	—2	3
—4	—5	—6	—4	—5	—6	—4	—5	—6
—7	—8	—9	—7	—8	—9	--7	—8	—9

TABLE V.—A.D. 1300 TO 1399.

MUSICAL EPOCHS AND EVENTS.

1300	* First principles of consonances and dissonances, by Marchettus.
1810	
1320	
1330	* Florid counterpoint ascribed to Jean de Mours.
1840	* Bands of *Weyghtes*, or Oboi, employed by Edward III.
1350	
1360	
1370	
1360	
1390	Masses, Motots, and other extended vocal compositions.

TABLE V.—A.D. 1300 TO 1399.

MUSICIANS.

1300 | —1 Marchettus —2 of Padua. | 1310 | 1320 | —3 | —4 | —5 Edward III. | —6 | Edward II. | —7 | —8 Jean de Meurs. 1330 | —9

Henry IV. | 1390 | 1360 | 1350 | 1340 | 1380 Dufay, b. | 1370 | Richard II.

TABLE VI.—A.D. 1400 TO 1499.

MUSICAL EPOCHS AND EVENTS.

1400	Rise of Belgian School.
1410	
1420	
1430	
1440	Early English School (Dunstable).
1450	* Development of Canonic or Fugal style.
1460	
1470	
1480	
1490	* The Organ Pedal introduced by Bernhardt at Venice.

TABLE VI.—A.D. 1400 TO 1499.

MUSICIANS.

1400	—1 *Dunstable b.	—2	—3	—4	—5	—6	—7	—8	—9

—10			—20			—30 * Hobrecht b. Dufay d. * Ockenheim b.		
—11	—12	—13 *Henry V.*	—1	—2 *Henry VI.*	—3	—1	—2	—3
—14	—15	—16	—4	—5	—6	—4	—5	—6
—17	—18	—19	—7	—8	—9	—7	—8	—9
—40 * J. des Pres b.			—50 Tinctor b.			—60		
—1	—2	—3	—1	—2	—3	—1 *Edward IV.*	—2	—3
—4	—5	—6	—4	—5	—6	—4	—5	—6
—7	—8	—9	—7	—8 Dunstable d.	—9	—7	—8	—9
—70			—80 Luther b. * Aaron b.			—90 * A. Willaert b. Walther b. Senfl b.		
—1	—2	—3	—1	—2	—3 *Edward V. Richard III.*	—1	—2	—3
—4	—5	—6	—4	—5 *Henry VII.*	—6	—4	—5	—6
—7	—8	—9	—7	—8	—9	—7	—8	—9

TABLE VII.—A.D. 1500 TO 1599.

MUSICAL EPOCHS AND EVENTS.

1500	Invention of Music-types, 1502.
1510	• Regals introduced.
1520	• Virginals in use : also the Viol family.
1530	Chorales in German Churches, in German tongue. Bassoon, 1539.
1540	
1550	• The MADRIGAL, ascribed to Willaert. Rise of "Italian School."
1560	Rise of Oratorio (St. Philip de Neri). Missa Papae Marcelli, 1565.
1570	• Violin introduced into England, 1577.
1580	Society of literati in Florence. Rise of Opera.
1590	• Serpent. Decline of the Belgian School. First Opera produced, 1594.

TABLE VII.—A.D. 1500 TO 1599.

MUSICIANS.

Arcadelt b. | Clement b. | Henry VIII.

1500 —1 —8 —9

—10 —20 —30 —40 —50 —60 —70 —80 —90

Goudimel b. | Morales b. | Tinctor d. | Lassus b. | Tye d. Senfl d. Vindana b. Vulpius b. Vittoria b. | White d. | Allegri b. | Carissimi b. | Zarlino d.

des Prés d. | Marbecke b. | Gallus (Händl) b. | Willaert d. | Farrant d. | Lossius d. | Gibbons b. | Gallus d.

Ockenheim d. | Mary | Clement d. Monteverde b. | Hassler b. De Rore | Schütz b. Marbecke d. Tallis d. | Palestrina d. Marenzio d. Lassus d. Waelrant d.

Palestrina b. | Tallis b. | Waltber d. | Frescobaldi b. | Carissimi b.

Waelrant b. | Zarlino b. | Elisabeth

G. Gabrieli b. | Lejeune b. | Marenzio b.

Byrde b. | Luther d.

Festa d. Eccard b.

Edward VI.

Arcadelt d.

Praetorius b. | Goudimel d.

TABLE VIII.—A.D. 1600 TO 1699.

MUSICAL EPOCHS AND EVENTS.

1600	Oratorio, *L'Anima è Corpo*, in Italy. Musicians' Company, founded 1604. Collection of Catches printed in England 1609.
1610	• Harpsichord introduced into England.
1620	First German Opera (*Daphne*), 1627.
1630	
1640	Rise of French Opera, 1645.
1650	French Opera: *La Pastorale*, Cambert, 1659.
1660	The *Arioso* introduced by Carissimi.
1670	*Psyche*, first English Opera, produced 1673. * Music (Copper) plates used in England. Macbeth Music, 1674. Purcell's *Dido and Eneas*, 1677.
1680	Purcell's 12 Sonatas for Violin, 1683.
1690	Purcell's *Te Deum*, 1694.

TABLE VIII.—A.D. 1600 TO 1699.

MUSICIANS.

1600	—1	—2	James I. —3	—4	—5	—6	Nanini d. —7	Child b. Vittoria d. —8	—9
Lawes b. Lejeune d.	—10		Lock b. —20				—30		
—11	G. Gabrieli d. —12	—13	Praetorius d. —1	Bull d. —2	Byrde d. —3		—1	—2	Lully b. —3
—14	—15	—16	—4	Viadana d. —5 Charles I. Gibbons d.	—6		—4	Lawes d. —5	—6
Vulpius d. —17	Hassler d. —18	—19	—7	—8	—9		—7	—8	—9
	—40		Monteverde d. —50				Lotti b. —60		Charles II.
Aldrich b. —1	—2	—3	—1	Allegri d. —2	—3		—1	—2	—3
—4	—5	—6	Frescobaldi d. —4	—5	—6		—4	—5	—6
—7	Blow b. —8	Common-wealth. —9	—7	Purcell b. —8	A. Scarlatti b. —9		—7	—8	—9
	—70		Marcello b. —80		William III. and Mary.			—90	
—1	Schütz d. Benevoli d. —2	Carissimi d. Keiser b. —3	—1	Bach b. James II. Handel b. —5	Rameau b. —3		—1	Tartini b. —2	—3
Caldara b. —4	—5	—6	Durante b. —4	—5	—6		Leo b. —4	Purcell d. —5	Child d. —6
Tock d. Croft b. —7	—8	—9	Wise d. Lully d. —7	—8	—9		—7	Greene b. —8	Hasse b. —9

TABLE IX.—A.D. 1700 TO 1799.

MUSICAL EPOCHS AND EVENTS.

1700 * Bassoon introduced into Orchestra. Italian Opera in England.

1710
Swell Organ, by Jordan, 1712.
Utrecht Te Deum, 1713.
* The Pianoforte (hammer-clavier) invented.

1720
Esther,—* first Oratorio in England.
Wohltemperirte Klavier, Vol. I., 1725.
* Clarinet.
Bach's Passion, 1729.

1730
* Invention of pedals to Harp.
Royal Society of Musicians, founded 1738.
Saul, Israel in Egypt, 1739.

1740
Messiah, 1741.
Samson, Dettingen Te Deum, 1743.

1750
Les Bouffons in Paris, 1752.
C. P. E. Bach's new fingering for Clavichord, 1753.

1760
* Pianoforte gradually supersedes the Harpsichord.
Gluck's Orfeo, 1764; Alceste, 1767.

1770
Many English Operas about this time.
Gluckists and Piccinists, 1776.

1780
* Corno di Bassetto, 1782.
Handel Commemoration, 1784.
Don Giovanni, 1787.

1790
Mozart's Requiem, 1791.
The Creation, 1798.

TABLE IX.—A.D. 1700 TO 1799.

MUSICIANS.

1700 — Graun b. — Anne.

Kent h.

Aldrich d. Boyce b. Arne b. Pergolesi b. —10

Blow d. Weldon b. —8

Clarke d. —7

—9

Cherubini b. —60

George III.

—90

Haydn b. —2 —1

Kent d. Weldon d. —6 —5 Sacchini b. —4

Arnold b. Marcello d. —9 Hatishill b. Pergolesi d. —8 —7

Mehul b. Caldara d. —3 —2 Dussek b. —1

Berton b. S. Wesley b. —6 Hummel b. —5 Rameau d. —4

—9 Romberg b. —8 —7

Rossini b. —3 —2 Herold b. Mozart d. —1

Benda d. —6 —5 Mosoholea b. Meyerbeer b. —4

—9 —8 Mercadante b. Donizetti b. Schubert b. —7

—30 —20

C. P. E. Bach b. —11

Jomelli b. George I. Gluck b. —14 Nares b. —15 —12 —16 —13

—17 —18 —19

Benda b. —3 —1 —2

Albrechtsberger b. —6 Scarlatti d. —5 —4

—9 J. A. Hiller b. Piccini b. —8 Croft d. George II. —7

—50 —40

Bach d. —1

D'Alayrac b. Viotti b. —3 Clementi b. —2

Mozart b. —6 Greene d. Durante d. —5 Cimarosa b. —4

Handel d. Graun d. —9 Travers d. —8 Pleyel b. —7

—80 —70

Nares d. Hasse d. —3 Auber b. Bishop b. —2 —1

Weber b. Sacchini d. —6 —5 Onslow h. Spontini b. Spohr b. —4

Fesca b. —9 —8 Gluck d. —7

Lotti d.

Gretry b. Naumann b. —1

Leo d. —6 —4 —5

—9 —8 —7

Beethoven b.

A. Reicha b. —3 —2 —1

Catel b. —6 Boieldieu b. Crotch b. —5 Jomelli d. —4

Boyce d. —9 Arne d. Hummel b. —8 Isonard b. —7

Tartini d.

TABLE X.—A.D. 1800 TO THE PRESENT TIME.

MUSICAL EPOCHS AND EVENTS.

1800	1810	1820	1830	1840	1850	1860	1870	1880	1890
Fidelio, 1805.		*Der Freischütz*, 1821. Royal Academy of Music founded, 1822. Beethoven's Choral Symphony, 1824.	*St. Paul*, 1836. English Operas by Balfe, Bishop, Benedict, &c.	*Elijah*, 1846. Royal Irish Acad. of Music, 1848.		College of Organists founded, 1864.	Trinity College, London, founded, 1872. Wagner's *Nibelungen*, 1876. National Training School for Music, opened 1876.		

TABLE X.—A.D. 1800 TO THE PRESENT TIME.

MUSICIANS.

—9	—8	—7	—6	—5	—4	—3	—2	—1	1800

Scale marks: —30, —20, —10, 1800, —40, —50, —60, —70

1800 — Goss b., Piccini d.

Battishill d., Naumann d. —1
Arnold d., Bellini b. —2
Berlioz b. —3
Benedict b., J. A. Hiller d. —4
Haydn d., D'Alayrac d., Mendelssohn b. —9

William IV.

Schumann b. — Costa b. — Chopin b. — Catel d. — *William IV.* — Herold d. —3, Brahms b. —6
—10
Liszt b. —11, Dussek d. —12, Gretry d. —13, Wagner b. — Ployel d., Joachim b. —1 — Clementi d. —2
Himmel d. —14, Verdi b. — Martini d. —16, Bennett b. — Boieldieu d. —4 — Bellini d. —5, Reicha d. —6
Mehul d. —17, Gade b. — Isouard d., Gounod b. —18, Hopkins b. —19 — S. Wesley d. —7, Himmel d., Victoria. — Attwood d. —8 — —9

George IV.

Schumann — Paganini d. — *George IV.* — Weber d., Fesca d. —6
—40
Cherubini d. —2, Berton d. —5 — Spontini d. —1, —4 — Romberg d. —1, Callcott d. — Ouseley b. —5 — Weber d., Fesca d. —6 —3
Crotch d., Mendelssohn d. —8 — Donizetti d. —8, Chopin d. —9 — Czerny d., W. Horsley d. —7 — Bishop d. —5, Schumann d. — Viotti d. —4 — Beethoven d. —7 — Schubert d. —8 — Spohr d. —9

Mercadante d., Balfe d., Moscheles d. —3 — Marx d.
—70
Auber d. —1, Fétis d. —2 — Rossini d. —8
Berton d. —4 — Dykes d. —6, S. Bennett d., S.S. Wesley d. — Berlioz d. —9
Titiens d. —8

6

SECTION III.—ART SUMMARY.

1. FOR the reasons adduced at the commencement of the first section of this work, we shall not lead our readers into the labyrinths of Greek scales, or the fanciful dissertations of mediæval writers on musical theory, but will proceed at once with the actual history of music as an art (and science), which practically dates from the fourth century after Christ.

2. The plain-song of the early Christian Church was, as we have seen, formed upon the old Greek scales or modes, the use of which was carried into Italy by the Greek slaves who acted as minstrels to the rich *dilletanti* of Rome. The voice was generally accompanied with the lyre (λύρα), an instrument which had from seven to fifteen or sixteen strings. Whether the lyre supplied harmony or merely "doubled" the voice is, however, an open question. There is no record of this instrument being employed in the Church; and in all probability it was judged as of too secular a character to admit of its use in Divine worship. The modes or scales of Gregory the Great have already been tabulated (*v. sect.* i. *par.* 10); we shall now present our readers with a view of the eight chants or "tones" formed upon those modes. The following are quoted by Sir John Hawkins from a work by Gaffurius (1502). For the convenience of the student we have translated them into the modern notation :—

Ex. 1. TABLE OF GREGORIAN TONES.

TONE I.

* Pri - mus   to - nus sic in - ci - pit sic me - dia - tur   et

---

* "The first Tone thus commenceth, thus proceedeth (or *mediates*), and thus endeth."

Ending i.   Ending ii.

sic fi - ni - tur . . . . . .

Ending iii.   Ending iv.

TONE II.

So - cun - dus to - nus sic in - ci - pit   sic me - di - a - tur

Ending i.   Ending ii.

et   sic   fi - ni - tur.

TONE III.

Ter - ti - us to - nus sic in - ci - pit   sic me - di - a - tur

Ending i.   Ending ii.   Ending iii.

et sic   fi - ni - tur.

TONE IV.

Quar - tus   to - nus sic in - ci - pit   sic me - di - a - tur

Ending i.   Ending ii.   Ending iii.

et   sic fi - ni - tur.

TONE V.

Quin - tus to - nus sic in - ci - pit   sic me - di - a - tur

Ending i.   Ending ii.

et   sic   fi - ni - tur.

Tone VI.

Sex - tus   to - nus sic in - ci - pit sic me - di - a - tur

et   sic . . . fi - ni -   tur.

Tone VII.   *Vel sic.*

Sep - ti - mus   to - nus   sic   in - ci - pit

Ending i.

et   sic . . . me - dia - tur   et sic fi - ni - tur.

Ending ii.   Ending iii.   Ending iv.

Tone VIII.   *Vel sic solennis.*

Oc - ta - vus   to - nus   sic   in - ci - pit

Ending i.   Ending ii.

sic   me - di - a - tur   et sic fi - ni - tur.

These chants were ordered to be used in all the
Christian churches of Europe, and to be used in their
integrity. It must not be supposed, however, that
strict uniformity in the manner of singing the tones

could be preserved throughout Christendom ; the Gallic singers took great liberties with the *Cantus firmus,* and were frequently rebuked for their many unpardonable licences. Besides the above, there were the more ancient "Ambrosian Chants," so called after St. Ambrose, who either composed them, or more probably directed their use in the Church. The following examples we take from Dr. Crotch's valuable work, " Specimens of Various Styles of Music ":—

Ex. 2. AMBROSIAN CHANTS. (*Circa* A.D. 334—397.)

3. The general method of singing the chants was alternate or antiphonal : either between priest or choir, or from "side to side," as the Psalms are now sung in our cathedrals. Cathedral choirs, and those of most churches, have for ages been divided into two portions facing each other, and respectively termed *Decani,* or the side of the Dean or other principal priest, and *Cantoris,* or the side of the Cantor, Precentor, or " chief singer." Hawkins mentions yet other modes of antiphonal singing :—" With respect to the music of the primitive church, though it consisted of psalms and hymns, yet was it performed in sundry different manners; that is to say, sometimes the psalms were sung by one person alone, the rest hearing with attention; sometimes they were sung by the whole assembly; sometimes alternately, the congregation being for that purpose divided into separate choirs; and, lastly, by one person, who repeated the first part of the verse, the rest joining in the close thereof. Of the four different methods of singing above enumerated, the second and third were very properly distinguished by the names of

symphony and antiphony, and the latter was sometimes
called responsaria ; and in this, it seems, women were
allowed to join, notwithstanding the apostle's injunction
on them to keep silence."

4. The ancient chants and hymn-melodies of the
Church were all built, as we have seen, upon the Greek
scales or modes—Dorian, Lydian, Phrygian, &c.   The
origin of the modern major scale, now common to the
whole of the civilized world, has never, to our knowledge, been actually traced or satisfactorily accounted
for.   The native airs of Western Europe, where the
modern scale took its rise, are built upon totally different tonalities—the Scotch and Irish, for instance ;
while in England itself, the primitive melodies sung by
rustics, from Yorkshire to Somerset, denote a mode
similar to, if not identical with, the Dorian.*   In the
absence of direct evidence to the contrary, we are inclined to the belief that our present scale was gradually evolved in obedience to the requirements of
counterpoint.   With most of the old modes the use of
imperfect concords (thirds or sixths), especially if
syncopated or suspended, would be less tolerable even
than sequences of consecutive fourths or fifths.   An
experiment upon a complete scalar passage in most
of the modes will exemplify this.   The absence of the
" leading-note "—the 7th of the scale a semitone distant
from the octave—for a long time deprived musicians of
the perfect cadence.   For one or two centuries after the
introduction of added parts to a melody, the subject
was invariably taken from the Gregorian plain-song ;
but gradually it became the custom to raise or lower by
a semitone various notes in order to avoid awkward intervals.   In the Dorian mode, for example, the sixth

---

* Many readers will doubtless recognize the following fragment
as a familiar "pastoral" strain :—

note, B♮, was altered to B♭, on account of the disso-
nance existing between the former note and F, the third
degree of the scale. If, to create a "leading-note,"
we raise the seventh degree (C♮) to C♯, we have at
once the complete modern scale of D minor. That
of D was the usual minor key with the early contrapuntists ; next to it came the key of A minor, possibly founded upon the related plagal mode, the Hypo-
Dorian (*v. sec. i. par.* 10), which required only the
raising of the seventh degree by a semitone to consti-
tute it a perfect modern minor scale.

5. The first attempt (on record) to clothe the bare
unisonal or octave-singing of the appointed plain chants
of the Church, was that of the Fleming, Hucbald. His
diaphony, or two-part accompaniment upon the rude
pipe-organ which at that time was being introduced into
the principal cathedrals of Europe, consisted of an un-
varying succession of fourths, fifths, or octaves, which
would give the *cantus firmus* a certain grimness and
stiffness not wholly out of character with the native
severity of the Gregorian tones. Some writers state that
the *organum* was not played but sung, others that it
was intended to be sung at a certain time-distance after
the *cantus*, as a kind of canonic imitation. But if we
look at the following specimen of the *organum* or
diaphony by Guido (*circa* 1022) we shall at once see
that the latter hypothesis is utterly untenable :—

Ex. 3. ORGANUM OR DIAPHONY.
(a) *Cantus.*

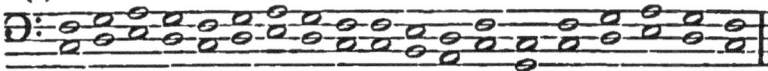

(β)

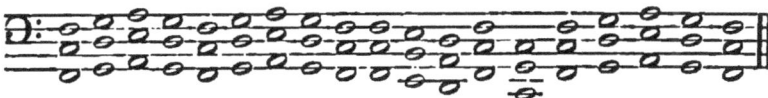

At whatever point we may commence the *discantus*
or under-part we shall be met, sooner or later, by in-

superable difficulties. We must, therefore, accept the
above crude accompaniment as it stands. We can,
however, imagine the birth of a more euphonious
counterpoint by the—perhaps at first—accidental combination of a portion of the *cantus firmus* with a new
commencement of the octave *organum,* as below :—

Ex. 4.
Cantus.

discantus.

At the point * the imitation would be interrupted,
when the performer would either resume his octave
accompaniment or proceed to the invention of further
imitations at other intervals. This suggestion is offered
with considerable diffidence and only in the absence of
any other rational proposition.

6. Into the various musical methods invented by, or
attributed to, Guido d'Arezzo, it would be impossible
to enter at length, in the present little work ; and many
of the descriptions, as given by Hawkins and others,
would only be confusing to the student. The chief
innovation appears to have been the extension of the
old tetrachordal system, introduced by Ambrose and
Gregory, to that of the hexachord, or six-note series.
This hexachord system is illustrated by the employment
of the UT, RE, MI, &c., which form the commencing
syllables of the lines we have already quoted (*sec.* i. 15) ;
the melody to which they are supposed to have been
set by Guido runs as follows :—

Ex. 5.

UT que - ant lax - is RE - so - na - re fi - bris

MI - ra ges - to-rum FA-mu - li tu - o - rum

SOL - ve pol-lu - ti LA-bi - i re - a - tum Sanc - te Jo-an-nes.

It will be observed that the tonality of this chant in no way coincides with that of our modern scale. The invention of the stave, or staff, for the purposes of notation, is popularly ascribed to Guido, though some writers affirm that a seven-lined stave * was in use before his time. For several centuries the size of the stave varied considerably, some employing three, some four, some seven, some eight, others ten, and others, again, as many as eleven lines. From the last mentioned it is stated that our modern five-lined staves are derived, the fixed F and C lines being variously supplemented above and below to suit the respective requirements of the various voices :—

Ex. 6.   Divisions of the Great Stave of Eleven lines.

Bass.   Baritone. Tenor. Alto.   Mezzo   Soprano. Violin or
                                Soprano.   G clef.

In the ancient missals the C and F lines were either painted in distinctive colours or were written as dotted or thickened lines, with a view to the more readily distinguishing them. They thus served, in a rude fashion, the purpose of the modern clefs, which, in their turn, are a development of the rudimentary forms to be seen in the staves still employed for "Gregorian" music :—

---

* Of this stave the lines only, not the spaces, were used for the notes.

Ex. 7.

F clef.   C clef.

This stave of four lines was the one generally adopted
in, and for some time after, the thirteenth century.

7. It would appear that Guido and his contemporaries used notes which were all of the same character
and relative time duration, for the first indication of
long and short notes we have is from the writings of
Franco of Cologne, who gives the *maxima, longa, brevis*
and *semibrevis (sec.* i. 16), and thus creates the *cantus
mensurabilis,* or measured song.   These characters and
terms were employed for several centuries, and our
modern system of notation is founded upon the invention of Franco.   For a long period the system was
ascribed to Jean de Meurs (or Muris), but the claim of
Franco has since been thoroughly established.   Dr.
Crotch furnishes the following specimen of Franco's
counterpoint, rendered into modern notation :—

Ex. 8.   FRANCO.

8. We advance a step in the history of counterpoint,
when we find Marchettus of Padua, who flourished
about the early part of the fourteenth century, giving
rules for the alternate employment of consonances and

dissonances. But if we are to place any faith in the authenticity of the preceding example—*i. e.* if it has not received some "finishing touches" from a later hand--we may be sure that nearly every rule necessary to the production of good counterpoint was known in the time of Franco.

9. The early theorists and historians generally were ecclesiastics, and devoted their attention mainly, if not exclusively, to Church music ; consequently there is but little record of the progress of secular music during the first twelve centuries after Christ. There are, however, various allusions to the existence of a race of itinerant minstrels, who visited the houses of the great, and sang to them ballads of which famous exploits or weird legends formed the principal themes. The story of King Alfred assuming the character of one of these wandering musicians, as a safe disguise and passport for admission into the enemy's camp, is a familiar passage in every history of England. There seems little doubt that Alfred was as accomplished a musician as he was a poet, and that he did much to further the progress of musical art in England. By some he is even credited with being the founder of the Chair of Music at Oxford, but there is scarcely sufficient evidence at hand to prove this. These "bards," or "troubadours," as they came to be called, led a romantic and adventurous life, and it was no uncommon freak for a man of gentle birth to take up the *rôle* for a time. Very frequently it so happened that two or more of these poet-minstrels were visiting the same house or hostelry at the same time, and as a natural consequence they entered into friendly competition for the first place in the esteem of their listeners. There is no doubt that this practice developed into the more public "tournaments of song" which formed a strong feature in the musical enterprise of the twelfth and thirteenth centuries. The *Minnesänger* were a famous confraternity of German troubadours who held public competitions for the post of

honour, or laureateship, of the country.   A notable con-
test of the Minnesänger took place about the year 1207,
in a town in Saxony.   It is affirmed that " the original
home of the troubadours was Provence, in the south of
France, where they originated about the eighth century.
Subsequently, at the time of the German Minnesänger,
there were also troubadours in Italy, Spain, and England."   The *Eisteddfod*, or annual musical competition
in Wales, is a remnant of the old bardic contests of
this country.   The Meistersänger of Germany were a
subsequent race of musicians, who in the fourteenth century sought to revive the ancient exploits of the Minnesänger, and for that purpose formed themselves into
bands or guilds for the regulation of contests ; but these
had a very ephemeral existence.   Wagner's opera the
Meistersinger is founded upon the popular traditions
regarding these later troubadours, who were, as a rule,
ignorant of the true art of poesy or of musical composition.

10. In the first section of this work (*par.* 17) we
have alluded to two or three of the principal troubadours of the thirteenth and fourteenth centuries, and
have given the first mention to Adam de la Hale, of
Provence.   In his " History of Music," Professor Ritter
gives two of De la Hale's melodies.   The second of
these two we shall quote here, with, however, a considerable alteration of Professor Ritter's added harmonies :—

Ex. 9.   Melody by De la Hale.

D. C. S.

The above is taken from a little musical play, or masque, entitled *Robin and Marion.* De la Hale composed several of these dramatic pieces, which were a kind of secular counterpart of the ancient miracle-plays or " mysteries "—of which more hereafter.

11. The art of counterpoint received its full development at the hands of the Belgian or Flemish masters, of whom Dufay was the first of any note. It was believed that to this master we owe the invention of the canon, or imitation at regular intervals of one voice by another. Here is a short canon in two parts, "at the octave above," by Dufay :—

Ex. 10.   DUFAY.

This specimen exhibits comparatively few crudities. The canon by Jusquin des Prés, of which the following is the commencement, is, however, a striking advance upon the work of Dufay :—

Ex. 11.   JUSQUIN DES PRÉS.

&c.

The musicians of this (and a later) period gloried in the production of canons, some of which were purposely so enigmatical that it taxed the ingenuity of their contemporaries to discover where they commenced, and at what intervals the various parts were to be employed. As in the poems of George Herbert we find him indulging in quaint metrical devices by which his lines are sometimes made to represent the shape of an altar or of wings, so we find the old contrapuntists moulding their canons into circles or triangles, or so contriving them that they may be sung any way—upside down, or backwards, making equally "good counterpoint" in either case. Most of these caprices must have cost their authors many months of labour and thought; but from a musical point of view they are worthless. As technical studies, however, they were not without a certain value, for they led to the discovery of the furthest resources at the musician's command, and familiarized him with every form of melodic combination.

12. The Belgian writers carried, as we have seen, the art of counterpoint* to great perfection, and formulated most of the rules which, with a few modifications, are observed by strict contrapuntists at the present day. They divided counterpoint into five principal methods or "species;" the first being note against note (the simplest and at the same time the most severe form); the second, two notes of counterpoint to one of the plain-song; the third, four notes to one; the fourth, syncopated counterpoint; and the fifth, figurate or florid counterpoint. For the benefit of the general reader a short illustration of each species of counterpoint is appended :—

Ex. 12. COUNTERPOINT (*first species*).

PLAIN-SONG, or CANTUS FIRMUS.

Ex. 13. COUNTERPOINT (*second species*).

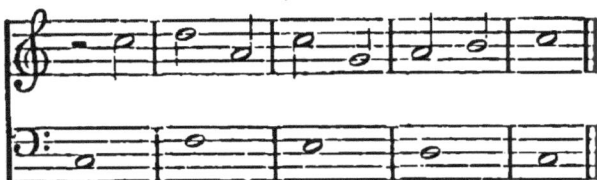

PLAIN-SONG.

Ex. 14. COUNTERPOINT (*third species*).

PLAIN-SONG.

---

* *Contra*, against; *punctum*, point, or note.

Ex. 15. COUNTERPOINT (*fourth species*).

PLAIN-SONG.

Ex. 16. COUNTERPOINT (*fifth species*).

PLAIN-SONG.

13. DESCANT was an art by which the singer was
able to add to a plain-song at sight a kind of rough
counterpoint consisting entirely of concords—the unison, third, fifth, sixth, and eighth. The early writers
laid down a number of rules as to the employment of
these intervals by the singer. The counterpoint in Ex.
12 would serve as an illustration of the allowed pro-
gression and intervals in descant. FABURDEN (or *falso
bordone*) was a yet simpler form of counterpoint, and
was originally, as the term indicates, nothing but a
drone bass, or "tonic pedal." The term was used
afterwards to signify a simplified species of descant,
moving, for the most part, in thirds or sixths. The
following fragment of an example given by Morley
will best show the nature of the faburden :—

Ex. 17. PLAIN-SONG.

FABURDEN.

3 1 3 3 3 3 3 1 3 3 3 3 1 3 3 3 1

The faburden, when written, was always placed *under* the plain-song.

14. In an earlier portion of this work (i. 24) we have alluded to the practice by the Belgian composers of employing the plain-song of the Church or the secular melody as the "given subject" on which to build their counterpoint. The first (so far as we know) to break through this established custom was Des Prés, who frequently invented his own subjects, and may be regarded as the first COMPOSER of modern music.*

15. It was not, however, until after the time of Palestrina that the ecclesiastical modes were entirely set aside for the modern major and minor scales. But Palestrina and his contemporaries had learnt to discard the circumscribed plain-song and the frivolous air, and—the former in an especial degree—gave to Church-music not only dignity but sweetness and expression.

16. The date of the introduction into the Church of music other than the liturgical (by liturgical music is understood the Mass, the setting of the Psalms and Canticles, &c.) is not precisely known. The *miracle-play*, which was the precursor of the **Oratorio**, was a very ancient institution, originally introduced by the ecclesiastical authorities as a means of popular instruction in sacred doctrine and history, but afterwards corrupted by the gradual introduction of absurd and monstrous traditions respecting our Saviour and his apostles, and by the interpolation of ludicrous soliloquies and dialogues. The reader may gain a very fair idea of these miracle-plays, or "mysteries," from the example which Longfellow gives in his well-known poem "The Golden Legend." *L'Anima e Corpo* (i. 33), produced as a specimen of the reform which St. Philip de Neri initiated in the sixteenth century, is little more than a "mystery" play, although it formed the immediate inau-

---

* The term "modern music" is used in contradistinction to that which existed in the ancient or ante-Christian periods.

guration of the oratorio. The stage-directions of Cavaliere, the composer of the music of *L'Anima e Corpo*, are
cited by Dr. Burney as follows :—" It is recommended
to place the instruments of accompaniment behind the
scenes,* which, in this first oratorio, were the following:
A double lyre, a harpsichord, a large or double guitar, and two flutes.—1. The words should be printed,
with the verses correctly arranged, the scenes numbered,
and characters of interlocutors specified.—2. Instead of
the overture, or symphony, to modern musical drama, a
madrigal is recommended, as a full piece, with all the
voice parts doubled, and a great number of instruments.
—3. When the curtain rises, two youths, who recite
the prologue, appear on the stage ; and when they
have done, *Time*, one of the characters in the Mo-
rality, comes on, and has the note with which he is
to begin given him by the instrumental performers
behind the scenes.—4. The *Chorus* are to have a place
allotted them on the stage, part sitting and part standing, in sight of the principal characters ; and when
they sing they are to rise and be in motion, with proper
gestures.—5. *Pleasure*, another imaginary character,
with two companions, are to have instruments in their
hands, on which they are to play while they sing and
perform the ritornels.—6. *Il Corpo*, the Body, when
these words are uttered, ' *Si che hormia alma mia*,'
&c., may throw away some of his ornaments, as his
gold collar, feather from his hat, &c.—7. The *World*,
and *Human Life* in particular, are to be gaily and richly
dressed ; and, when they are divested of their trappings,
to appear very poor and wretched, and at length dead
carcases.—8. The symphonies and ritornels may be
played by a great number of instruments ; and, if a
violin should play the principal part, it would have
a good effect.—9. The performance may be finished with

---

* It is noticeable that Wagner has reverted to this old practice
of concealing the orchestra.

or without a dance.   If without, the last chorus is to be doubled in all its parts, vocal and instrumental ; but if a dance is preferred, a verse beginning thus : ' *Chiostri altissimi, e stellati,*' is to be sung, accompanied sedately and reverentially by the dance.   Then shall succeed other grave steps, and figures of the solemn kind. During the ritornels the four principal dancers are to perform a ballet, '*saltato con capriole,*' enlivened by capers or *entrechats,* without singing, and thus, after each stanza, always varying the steps of the dance ; and the four principal dancers may sometimes use the *galiard,* sometimes the *canary,* and sometimes the *courant* step, which will do very well in the ritornels.* —10. The stanzas of the ballet are to be sung and played by all the performers within and without." This description, which presents to the mind a thing totally foreign to the modern idea of an oratorio performance, is valuable as showing that the original intention of the promoters was to establish a sacred drama, not a lengthy religious cantata, under the title " oratorio."   But very few of the oratorios which are popular at the present day are literally dramatic.   The *Messiah* or the *Creation* could not possibly be adapted to the stage without mutilation.   On the other hand Bach's *Passion* (that of *St. Matthew* in particular) would seem to approach very nearly to the old idea of the oratorio, a sacred musical drama, with its narrator, and the responsive double choirs.

17. It will be seen that the early oratorio was constituted of the recitative, the chorus, and the *ritornello* or instrumental interlude.   The recitative, or *musica parlante,* introduced as a revival of the old Greek form of musical declamation, was employed chiefly as a vehicle for the narrative portions of the sacred play.   It was usually sung to the accompaniment of the theorbo (arch-lute) or of the spinnet or harpsichord.   Cavaliere in oratorio, and Monteverde in opera, effected some

* *Ritornello,*—an interlude or *entr' acte.*

improvements upon the original crude *recitativo*, but Carissimi gave it an established form; and the *Arioso* sprang out of these continued elaborations. The *Aria*, with its "binary" construction, was a still later development. The following example of recitative is taken from Mr. Leslie's edition of Carissimi's oratorio, *Jonah* :—

Ex. 18.   Recitative from *Jonah.*   Carissimi.

And there-up-on they cast lots, and be-hold the

lot did fall up-on Jo - nah.   So all the men who were

a tempo moderato.

in the ship said un - to him.

A short extract from the same oratorio will serve as a fair illustration of the dramatic chorus-music of the seventeenth century :—

Ex. 19.   Chorus from *Jonah.*   CARISSIMI.

So they did take up   Jo - nah, and did did cast him forth in - to the

sea,   and the sea did then cease from the   fu-ry of   its   rag-ing.

What has been said of the art-development of the oratorio will apply also to the opera. There is indeed but little distinction to be made between "sacred" and "secular" choral music of those days. The following chorus from an opera by Caccini will show this :—

Ex. 20.   CACCINI.

&c.

Until about the middle of the eighteenth century, oratorio took its place as Church music, *i. e.* it was regarded as an adjunct to, if not indeed an important feature of, Divine worship. Hence the introduction, by Bach, into his Passion Music, of familiar chorales in which the congregation were allowed to take part. Mendelssohn, who was an ardent admirer of Bach, and was mainly instrumental in reviving the popularity of that great master, himself introduces old chorales in his oratorio, *St. Paul*, and also in the *Lobgesang*, which was first performed in the Church of St. Thomas, Leipsic. It was Handel who established the oratorio upon the secular stage, and since his time performances of oratorio have been almost universally confined to the concert-room. Very recently, however, there has been a movement in favour of reinstating this class of music in its original place, and the *Passions* of Bach, and other oratorios, or lengthy selections from them, are now frequently performed in our cathedrals and larger churches. In design and construction, the development of the oratorio progressed side by side with that of other departments of musical art; and save in the matter of orchestration, this species of composition is pretty much where Bach left it. It only remains, therefore, to append a list, chronologically arranged as far as possible, of the principal composers of oratorio, to whose names, occurring in the first section of this work, the reader is referred for further information :—

Name.	*Principal Works.*
Cavaliere (1600),	*L'Anima e Corpo.*
Carissimi (1530—1673),	*Jonah ; Jephtha,* &c.
Schütz (1585—1672),	*Passion ; Resurrection,* &c.
Keiser (1673—1739),	*Bleeding and Dying Jesus.*
J. S. Bach (1685—1750),	*Passion (S. Matthew & S. John).*
Handel (1685—1759),	*Messiah, Israel in Egypt,* &c.
Leo (1694—1746),	*Death of Abel.*
Graun (1701—1759),	*Der Tod Jesu.*
Stradella (c. 1750),	*St. John the Baptist.*

Name.	Principal Works.
Haydn (1732—1809),	*Creation : Seasons.*
Crotch (1775—1847),	*Palestine ; Captivity.*
Beethoven (1770—1827),	*Mount of Olives.*
Spohr (1784—1859),	*Calvary ; Last Judgment,* &c.
Mendelssohn (1809—1847),	*Elijah ; St. Paul.*

Among the composers of oratorio of our own day may be mentioned : Macfarren (*St. John the Baptist,* &c.); Costa (*Eli ; Naaman*); Benedict (*St. Peter*); Ouseley (*St. Polycarp ; Hagar*); Sullivan (*Prodigal Son ; Light of the World*). The exquisite sacred cantata of the late Sterndale Bennett (*The Woman of Samaria*) may justly be classed with the oratorio.

18. The **Mass**, a species of composition called forth by the requirements of the Roman liturgy, is of very early date, and may be divided into two classes : the first, *Missa Solemnis,* sung at high celebrations of the Holy Eucharist ; the second, *Requiem,* used at Masses for the Dead. The *Missa Solemnis* generally consists of the following separate movements : *Kyrie Eleison, Gloria in Excelsis* (usually subdivided into *Gloria, Domine Deus, Quoniam Tu Solus,* &c.). *Credo in unum Deum* (again subdivided into *Credo, Et Incarnatus,* &c.), *Sanctus, Benedictus, Agnus Dei.* The Requiem Mass contains, in addition to the liturgical numbers, — the *Gloria,* however, being usually omitted, — the beautiful Latin hymn known as the *Dies Iræ.* It is seldom that the whole of the *Dies Iræ* is included in the *Requiem,* as the performance of an elaborate setting of every verse would be too wearisome. The verses most commonly selected are *Dies Iræ, Tuba mirum, Recordare,* and *Lachrymosa.* At first the Mass was sung to an authorized plain-song, which, as the art of counterpoint developed, gradually came to be accompanied by other voice-parts, above and below. Then new melodies, many of them being, as we have seen, popular secular tunes of the period, were introduced as subjects upon which the contrapuntist might exercise his ingenuity in constructing canonic imitations, and so-

called fugues (i. 24). This abuse of the art having
been denounced by the Council of Trent, Palestrina at
once effected wonderful reform by means of his noble
Masses, of which we have already given some account
(i. 29)   For a long period Masses were sung without
any kind of instrumental accompaniment; a primitive
kind of orchestration was, however, introduced towards
the close of the sixteenth century. Since the Reformation, English composers have had no opportunity of
distinguishing themselves by setting the " Mass." The
Communion Office of the English Church is ill-adapted
to an elaborated musical treatment. The *Kyrie Eleison*
is only a short response repeated after each Command-
ment ; the *Benedictus* and *Agnus Dei*, though still used
without authority in some churches, are unusual subjects;
while the remainder cannot be split up into detached
movements. The single-voice setting known as Merbecke's is an adaptation of a traditional plain-song, with
a number of interpolations by Merbecke himself. In
Roman Catholic Churches the Mass has always been
the principal function ; consequently every known resource has at all times been employed to give grandeur
and solemnity to this portion of the Roman liturgy.
The compositions of Mozart, Haydn, Beethoven, Schubert, and other modern composers were therefore arranged for soli, chorus, and full orchestra.* The principal composers of this form of work are very numerous,
and in the following list we do not attempt to include
other than the most notable amongst them :—

> Dufay (1380—1430).
> Ockenheim (1430—1513).
> Des Prés (1440—1521).
> Palestrina (1514—1594).
> Lassus (1520—1595).
> Byrde (1543—1623).
> Allegri (1580—1652).

---

* At St. Peter's, Rome, however, no instrumental accompaniment
of any sort is permitted.

Scarlatti (1659—1725).
Fux (1660—1732).
Caldara (1678—1763).
Marcello (1680—1739).
Bach (1685—1750).
Leo (1694—1746).
Durante (1693—1755).
Fco (1699—1750).
Hasse (1699—1783).
Pergolesi (1710—1736).
Graun (1701—1759).
Haydn (1732—1809).
Webbe (1740—1816).
Paesiello (1741—1816).
Naumann (1741—1816).
Martini (1741—1816).
Zingarelli (1752—1837).
Mozart (1756—1791).
Cherubini (1760—1842).
Beethoven (1770—1827).
Hummel (1778—1837).
Weber (1786—1826).
Rossini (1792—1868).
Schubert (1797—1828).
Berlioz (1803—1869).

19. But while the English School was deprived of
so complete a subject—from a musical point of view—
as the Mass, the purified liturgy of the Anglican
Church still afforded the musician ample scope for the
exhibition of his imagination and skill. There yet remained to him the *Te Deum, Magnificat,* and other
Canticles, the Psalms and Hymns, and that other important item, peculiar to the Church of England, the
Anthem.

20. The **Anthem** was always regarded as the principal
feature of the English " Cathedral Service," as it could be
elaborated at the will of the composer, and was generally
of two or more movements. The words of Anthems
are, as a rule, taken from Scripture ; but sometimes
portions of the Prayer Book (the Collects for instance)
have been used. *Verse Anthems* are such as contain

one or more movements assigned to a single voice, or to a duet, trio, or quartet; usually concluding with a chorus.   There are many instances, however, of verse Anthems in which the only movements are for solo voices.   *Full Anthems* are those in which the whole choir may take part throughout.   *Verses* are of very frequent occurrence in Anthems and Service-music, as Church composers were naturally desirous of displaying the leading voices in the Cathedral or other Church choirs under their charge.   Some of these "verses" are very elaborate—almost to tediousness ; a fair specimen of this kind of anthem is *I was in the Spirit,* by Dr. Blow.   The "verse" parts in Cathedral music, with the exception of solos, are generally sung without accompaniment, while the "full" portions, or choruses, are accompanied by an organ-part, sometimes independent, but more usually a mere "doubling" of the voices. Most of the following composers of Anthems have also written Service-music, *i. e.* settings of the Canticles and Communion Office ; and what we have said about the Anthem applies also to the Service-music of our Cathedrals.*

Names.	*Anthems.*
Tye (1500—1560),	†*I will exalt Thee,* &c.
Tallis (1523—1585),	†*I call and cry,* &c.
Byrde (1543—1623),	†*Bow down Thine ear.*
Gibbons (1583—1625),	†*Hosanna to the Son of David,* &c.
Child (1608—1696),	†*Praise the Lord, O my Soul.*
Blow (1648—1708),	†*I beheld, and lo,* &c.

---

* The student is recommended to procure as many as he can of the Anthems here enumerated ; and if he study them in their chronological order he will gain a better insight than any verbal description will give him, into the development of form and style, as well as the individual characteristics of each composer.

† Anthems thus marked have been published (or republished) within a recent date, and are easily procurable.

Names.	Anthems.
Wise (*d.* 1687),	*Prepare ye the way.*
Purcell (1658—1695),	†*O give thanks.*
Clark (*d.* 1707),	†*I will love Thee.*
Aldrich (1647—1710),	†*O Praise the Lord.*
Croft (1677—1727),	†*God is gone up.* &c.
Greene (1698—1755),	†*O Clap your hands.*
Kent (1700—1736),	†*Hear my prayer.*
Handel (1685—1759),	*Chandos Anthems.*
Weldon (1708—1736),	†*Hear my crying.*
Boyce (1710—1779),	†*By the waters of Babylon.*
Travers (*d.* 1758),	†*Ascribe unto the Lord.*
Nares (1715—1783),	†*Blessed is he that considereth.*
Battishill (1738—1801),	†*Call to Remembrance.*
Arnold (1739—1802),	†*Who is this that cometh.*
S. Wesley (1766—1837),	†*Thou, O God, art praised.*
Crotch (1775—1847),	†*How dear are Thy counsels.*
Attwood (1767—1838),	†*Come, Holy Ghost.*
Clarke-Whitfeld,	†*Behold, how good and joyful.*
Mendelssohn (1809—1847),	†*Judge me, O God.*
Walmisley,	†*Father of Heaven.*
SterndaleBennett(1816—1875),	†*O that I knew.*
S. S. Wesley (*d.* 1876),	†*The Wilderness.*
Dykes (*d.* 1876),	†*These are they.*

Among the most prominent writers of Anthems and Service-music in the present day are, Goss, E. J. Hopkins, Macfarren, Ouseley, Elvey, Sullivan, Stainer, Stewart, Steggall, Turle, Barnby, Bridge, Calkin, Garrett, Smart, Thorne, and Tours. Some modern Anthems have been scored for full orchestra, and are more dramatic and descriptive in style than those of the older writers.

21. Many pages might be taken up with the history of the Hymn-tune, or **Chorale**, a species of composition which, because it is easily learned by ear, becomes the special property of the people, and like an heirloom, is handed from generation to generation. Many "Gregorian" hymn-tunes are in use at the present day, and it is needless to say that they are of the most ancient date ; but their presence in the hymnals of our day is

due, not to their having been treasured up by the masses, but to the zeal of a few musical antiquarians. Of these about the best are *Urbs beata, Jesu dulcis memoria,* and *Corde natus,* named respectively after the first words of the Latin hymns to which they were composed. Ex. 17 (par. 13) will show the commencement of an ancient tune very familiar to those accustomed to the use of a certain Church hymnal.* The scales in which these old melodies are written are ill-suited to the modern process of harmonization, and the vocal harmonies added to many of these "Gregorian" tunes are necessarily forced and disconnected, leaving no impression of a distinct tonality — they are, in short, without beginning and without end. For many of the old tunes which are really and truly the heritage of the English and German nations we are indebted to the great religious movement of the sixteenth century under Luther, who, with the aid of Walther and Goudimel, published the first collection of chorales to words in the vernacular (1524). The two chorales, *Ein' feste burg ist unser Gott (a strong tower is our God),* and *Great God, what do I see and hear,* are both ascribed to Luther, but it is doubtful whether he really composed them, though he may have arranged or harmonized them for Walther's book, probably with some help from Goudimel or Clemens non Papa. "The Old Hundredth" has been variously ascribed to Luther, to Goudimel, and to Guillaume Franc; all that is positively known concerning this immortal tune is that it was published about the year 1550. It is by no means improbable, however, that it had actual existence, either "orally" or in manuscript, even before that date. Many of these ancient hymn-tunes were doubtless quotations or adaptations from larger works. Tallis's Canon, well-known in our time in connection with the Evening Hymn, belongs to this class :

---

* *Hymns Ancient and Modern.*

Ex. 21. TALLIS.

The canon, "at the octave below," is between the treble and tenor voices, and these parts are given in larger notes for the sake of distinctness. The other two parts serve to complete the harmony. Moreover, if the experiment be tried, it will be found that the Old Hundredth can be made, with only three alterations (marked *), to form a crude kind of "canon, two in one at the octave below," at the half-bar distant :

Ex. 22. OLD HUNDREDTH.

It will also be observed that this "canon" is infinite

or perpetual, on examining the two points ‡ ‡. The
alterations (* and **) might easily be accounted for.
That such a combination, crude as it is, will be regarded
in the light of a mere coincidence, we can hardly anti-
cipate. The fact that many of the old masters were
accustomed to take fragments of chorales as subjects for
fugal writing, would seem to prove that these ancient
melodies were often originally composed with a view to
canonic imitation, more or less strict, in the accom-
panying voices. We might multiply instances, but
the following fragments will suffice for our present
purpose :

Ex. 23.   (From the *Würtemberger Gesangbuch*—1583 [?].)

(a) at 8ve below.

(β) at 8ve below.

Esslingen.   KRIEGER (c. 1650).

(γ) at 8ve above.

KÖLNER GESANGBUCH.

(δ) at 4th below.

Our modern hymn-tunes are in too many cases characterized by a straining after vivid effects in harmony, to the exclusion of the flowing counterpoint which gives an unmistakable grace and dignity to the old chorale. It is unnecessary to attempt to catalogue the names of composers of hymn-tunes; the best amongst our English writers will be found amongst the composers of anthems mentioned in the preceding paragraph.

22. We now pass into the dominion of secular music. After the "folk-songs" of the troubadours, which had a long and uncontested popularity for many ages, came the **Madrigal,** a kind of part-song, about the precise origin of which there has been a great deal of useless speculation. The term "madrigal" has been variously accounted for, some opining that it comes from *madre di gala,* or "mother of the festival"—in allusion to the Virgin Mary as patron of the month of May, with its olden pastoral festivities; others that the name is derived from that of the Spanish town, Madrigal, where one, Don Jorge, an early writer of "madrigal" poetry, lived, and whence, after the fashion of those days, he derived his surname, "de Madrigal." Other theories have been advanced, but they are not even worth mentioning; the most feasible is that which assigns the term to the above prolific and popular writer of madrigal poetry; for it has been in all ages the custom to associate a thing with the name of a noted producer. The earliest form of madrigal, but for the secular words—generally of a pastoral, or an amorous character—could hardly be distinguished from the sacred motett, or anthem. There is little doubt, moreover, that for a long period the madrigal was written for voices only—it was a chorus, in fact, with-

out instrumental accompaniment. The madrigal composers of the Elizabethan era greatly developed and
extended this form of composition, freely employing
canonic imitation, and other contrapuntal devices. The
ancient " Ballets " and " Fa las " were also a species of
madrigal, but were usually of a more light and trifling
kind, and bore little resemblance in form to the madrigal proper. Some historians have assigned the introduction of the madrigal to Adrian Willaert, chapel-
master of St. Mark, Venice, but this is uncertain ; at
all events it is known that his successor at St. Mark's,
Cyprian de Rore, devoted himself to this form of
composition, and gained a high reputation for it. The
latter part of the sixteenth century was the golden age
of the madrigal, particularly in England, under the
reign of Elizabeth, who fostered music no less than the
other liberal arts. *The Triumphs of Oriana*, dedicated
to Queen Elizabeth, is the finest collection of madrigals
extant (i. 27). The best of these are popular even in
the present day. Luca Marenzio, a friend of Dowland,
was one of the most accomplished among the many
Italian madrigalists of the sixteenth century. The
madrigal, *Dissi a l'amata*, quoted *in extenso* by both
Hawkins and Crotch, opens as follows :—

Ex. 24.   MARENZIO.

The above is a compression of the vocal score; the
madrigal pure was not accompanied as a rule, though
indeed there are many madrigals extant with *basso
continuo,* or bass figured for lute or harpsichord. The
modern "madrigal" is hardly distinguishable from the
"part-song;" *i. e.* it contains a continuous melody, and
is generally provided with a pianoforte accompaniment.
The following is a sufficiently comprehensive list of the
chief madrigal composers, and the madrigals mentioned are those of especial note at the present day :—

Name.	*Madrigal.*
Willaert [?] (1490—1563),	
Festa (*d.* 1545),	*Quando ritrovo (Down in a flowery vale).*
De Rore (*c.* 1580).	
Palestrina (1514—1594).	
R. Edwardes (1520—1566),	*In going to my lonely bed.*
Marenzio (1550—1594),	*Dissi a l'amata.*
Byrde (1543—1623),	*While the bright sun.*
Wilbye (1560—1612),	*Flora gave me fairest flowers.*
Dowland (1562—1626),	*Awake, sweet love.*
Morley (1563—1604),	*My bonny lass.*
Benet (1565—1605),	*Ye restless thoughts.*
Gibbons (1583—1625),	*Oh that the learned poets.*

After Gibbons the madrigal deteriorated, and though T. Linley, W. Horsley, W. Callcott, and R. L. Pearsall have contributed some excellent models, this species of composition may be regarded as belonging to the past.

23. The **Glee** was an offshoot, or, more correctly, a later development of the madrigal. While the latter consisted of only one movement, the glee had two, three, and four. The glee was also written for solo voices in each part, and therefore was capable of much greater style and finish than the madrigal, which was designed for the chorus. In the present day the glee is more popular than its precursor, doubtless because the style of the former is in greater accordance with the requirements of modern art. The glee is now frequently sung by modern choral societies, by which means, although some of these bodies are highly trained and capable of putting great expression into the music they sing, the real charm of the glee is lost. At one time Rounds and Catches were the most popular "domestic music" in vogue, and many of these catches were, in fact, glees in which a punning expression was given to the words. To this day glees are divided into two kinds—the serious and the cheerful—though the latter does not necessarily imply a playing upon words. The father of the English glee was Thomas Brewer, whose *Turn Amaryllis* is still a favourite at the glee-clubs. The writers of glees have been so numerous that we cannot give more than the leading glee-composers in the following list :—

Name.	*Glees.*
T. Brewer (1609—1676),	*Turn Amaryllis.*
T. Arne (1710—1778).	*Which is the properest day, &c.*
S. Webbe (1740—1816),	*When winds breathe soft.*
Stafford Smith (1750—1836),	*Blest pair of sirens.*
R. J. S. Stevens (1723—1837),	*Sigh no more, ladies.*
Dr. Callcott (1766—1821),	*The Red Cross Knight.*
R. Spofforth (1770—1827),	*Hail, smiling morn.*

Name.	Glees.
W. Horsley (1774—1858),	*By Celia's Arbour.*
Sir H. Bishop (1782—1855),	*I gave my Harp.*
Sir J. Goss (*b.* 1800),	*Ossian's Hymn to the Sun.*

24. Our first section contains a brief account of the rise of the **Opera** (par. 32), and, so far as it goes, there is little to add here. It is to be noticed, however, that many composers of later periods considered the subjects of the primitive operas worthy of further experiment. *Dafne*, *Euridice*, and *Orfeo* have received new interpretations since the times of Peri, Caccini, and Monteverde—the *Daphne*, for instance, of Schütz and of Handel, and the *Orfeo* of Gluck. From the year 1594, the date of the production of Peri's *Dafne*, to the year 1627, the opera appears to have been confined exclusively to Italy, its native home. In 1627, however, Schütz' *Daphne* formed the introduction of opera into Germany, which has since done so much for this branch of the art. In 1645 *Italian* opera was introduced into France under the auspices of Cardinal Mazarin, but the first French opera was that of Cambert (*La Pastorale*), composed in 1659. England follows very closely upon France, for in 1673 was produced the *Psyche* of Lock.

25. A complete, though concise, history of the opera would fill a volume like the present, and an account of Italian opera alone would occupy three-fourths of the space. Our remarks upon Italian opera must therefore be very sparing, and we shall not unnecessarily repeat any statements made in former sections, which may be readily referred to upon occasion by means of the General Index. From the date of its inauguration under Peri and Caccini, the opera in Italy has not ceased, up to the present day, to keep pace with the general progress of the art. The vocal features of the opera are now, and have always been,— as in the case of the oratorio,—the recitative, the aria,

the duet (and occasionally the trio, quartet, quintet, &c.), and the chorus.* The instrumental accompaniments, the overture, and the interludes (*entr'actes*) or symphonies, were also in the earlier days of the opera very similar to those of the oratorio. By degrees, however, the similarity to the oratorio as regards both style and treatment became less and less, and at this time the oratorio and the opera have little in common. It is in the works of Monteverde that the first signs of a greater freedom in the treatment of secular subjects are apparent; witness the following extracts—portions of recitative and duet from his *Orfeo :—*

Ex. 25.   (*Apollo descends in a cloud, singing.*)   MONTEVERDE.

Perch' a   lo sdegno   ed al do - lor in pre - da   Co -

si ti do-nio fig - lio? Non è non è con-sig-lio? &c.

Ex. 26.   (*Apollo and Orfeo ascend to heaven, singing.*) MONTEVERDE.

Saliam,   .   .   .   Saliam,   .   .   .

Saliam,   .   .   .

* Even the Chorale has been introduced, when suited to the scene or occasion.

After Monteverde, the next great light of the Italian opera was A. Scarlatti, known as the founder of the so-called Neapolitan School. His operas, *Carlo Re d'Almagna*, *Il Ciro*, and others, were an immense advance upon their predecessors, and obtained for him the first place among the opera-composers of his day. His style would now be considered stilted and conventional, but they have decided form, and mark an epoch in the development of the aria. Lotti and Sacchini were the immediate successors of Scarlatti,

while Piccini was, as we know, the favoured champion
of the Italian school in France.   Gluck, Hasse, Mozart,
and other German composers contributed largely, if
not mainly, to Italian opera; while Handel, German
as he was by nationality, was essentially Italian in
opera.   Gluck in his later operas (i. 45, 46), such as
Orfeo and *Alceste,* was the first to break from the established lines, and the *Zauberflöte* of Mozart is generally
looked upon as the pioneer of a distinct German school
of musical drama.   The little-known *Euryanthe* of
Weber is still more decidedly " German," but Richard
Wagner has gone beyond all others in the noted
"Tetralogy" of 1876.   Wagner has initiated a complete revolution in opera, discarding the set airs, and
substituting for them a modernized *musica parlante,*
or recitative.   He declines to write melodies for the
purposes of mere vocal display.   The old traditions as
to the "related keys" are cast aside without com-
punction.   In short he makes music entirely subservient
to the dramatic element.   With him, the *libretto* is
no longer a species of lay figure upon which to hang
any kind of musical drapery or embroidery that the
composer may fancy or the singer desire.   Wagner
composes his own libretti, and this fact illustrates the
fundamental principle on which he works, and of
which he is so strenuous an advocate.   This principle
is, that the music, the poetry, and the *mise-en-scène* of
an opera should each aid, not over-weight the other,
and thus unite to produce the desired dramatic effect.
The old opera may be regarded, on the other hand, as
a collection of vocal and instrumental compositions or
numbers, each complete in itself as to form, and
strung together by the story of the libretto.   In fact,
Wagner's dramatic music is so far removed from that
which for ages has been known as "opera," that it has
been difficult for musicians or the public to connect the
former with the latter.   They therefore say "this is
not opera," and some few add "nor even music."   It is,

however, to be remembered that no musician has ever ventured upon a new path without bringing upon himself and his work the doubt, suspicion, or contempt of the majority of his contemporaries, who are naturally satisfied with what their predecessors and themselves have done. In such cases it is posterity which assigns to a musician or thinker (a composer must be both) his rightful place in the realm of art. If we view the subject from Wagner's new standpoint, all previous opera can only be regarded as of the Italian type, whether produced by Italian, German, French, or English composers. Thus, the operas of Purcell, though the words are English, were avowedly constructed upon Italian models, and the same may be said of the works of every English composer of opera, from Lock to Balfe. In short, the success of the English composer has been in proportion to his power of assimilation to the Italian style. To the French composers, from Cambert to Gounod, though many splendid works have been produced, we may apply the same terms. Germany, however, may claim the honour of effecting most of the improvements which are now universally accepted as essentials. Gluck's *Orfeo*, Mozart's *Zauberflöte*, Weber's *Euryanthe*, Wagner's *Lohengrin*, are so many landmarks in the development of opera; and such a view is not inconsistent with the conviction that the works of Purcell or Handel in the past, and of Verdi or Gounod in the present are important contributions to musical art. The following are the most celebrated opera-composers of every school, and further information respecting each may be gained on reference (by means of the General Index) to the name wherever it occurs in our first section :—

Name.	*Principal Works.*
Peri (*c.* 1600),	*Dafne.*
Caccini (*c.* 1600),	*Euridice.**

* Jointly with Peri.

Name.	Principal Works.
Monteverde (1566—1650),	*Orfeo, Arianna*, &c.
Schütz (1585—1672),	*Daphne.*
Cambert (*c.* 1659),	*La Pastorale.*
Lock (1620—1677),	*Psyche.**
Lully (1633—1687),	*Tragédies Lyriques.*
Henry Purcell (1658—1695),	*Dido and Æneas, King Arthur,* &c.
Lotti (1660—1740),	*Various.*
A. Scarlatti (1659—1725),	*Carlo Re d'Almagna.*
Keiser (1673—1739),	*More than* 100 *operas.*
Rameau (1683—1764),	*Castor and Pollux.*
Handel (1685—1759),	*Almira, Rinaldo*, &c.
Leo (1694—1745),	*Olympiade.*
Hasse (1699—1783),	*Various.*
Clayton (*c.* 1700),	*Arsinoë, Rosamund.*
Graun (1701—1759),	*Various.*
Pergolesi (1710—1736),	*Various.*
Arne (1710—1778),	23 *Operas* (*Artaxerxes*, &c.).
Boyce (1710—1779),	*The Chaplet.*
D'Auvergne (1713—1797),	*Les Troqueurs.*
Gluck (1714—1787),	*Orfeo, Alceste, Armide*, &c.
Benda (1722—1795),	*Ariadne auf Naxos, Medea.*
J. A. Hiller (1728—1804),	*Liederspiele.*
Piccini (1728—1800),	*Roland,* &c.
Monsigny (1729—1817),	*Rose et Colas, Le Deserteur.*
Arnold (1739—1802),	40 *English Operas.*
Grétry (1741—1813),	*Zemire et Azor*, &c.
D'Alayrac (1753—1809),	*Les Deux Savoyards.*
Mozart (1756—1791),	*Don Giovanni, Figaro, Zauberflöte*, &c.
Cherubini (1760—1842),	*Les Deux Journées. Medea*, &c.
Storace (1763—1796),	14 *English Operas.*
Mehul (1763—1817),	*Joseph, Euphrosyne.*
Himmel (1765—1814),	*Fanchon.*
Berton (1766—1844),	*Ponce de Leon,* &c.
Beethoven (1770—1827),	*Fidelio* (*Leonora*).
Catel (1773—1830),	*Sémiramis.*
Boieldieu (1775—1834),	*La Dame Blanche.*
Isouard (1777—1818),	*Cendrillon.*

---

* The celebrated "Macbeth Music" has recently been claimed for Purcell.

Name.	Principal Works.
Auber (1782—1871),	*Fra Diavolo, Masaniello.*
Sir H. Bishop (1782—1855),	*Miller and his men,* &c.
Spohr (1784—1859),	*Faust, Jessonda.*
Spontini (1784—1851),	*La Vestale.*
Weber (1786—1826),	*Der Freischütz, Preciosa, Euryanthe.*
Herold (1791—1833),	*Zampa.*
Rossini (1792—1868),	*Guglielmo Tell, Semiramide,* &c.
Meyerbeer (1794—1864),	*Les Huguenots, L'Africaine.*
Schubert (1797—1828),	*Rosamunde* (incidental music).
Donizetti (1797—1868),	*Lucrezia Borgia, Lucia,* &c.
Halevy (1799—1862),	*La Juive, Les Mousquetaires.*
Bellini (1802—1835),	*Norma, La Sonnambula.*
Berlioz (1803—1869),	*Benvenuto Cellini.*
Sir J. Benedict (*b.* 1804),	*Gipsy's Warning, Lily of Killarney.*
Balfe (1808—1870),	*Bohemian Girl, Talisman.*
Mendelssohn (1809—1847),	*Wedding of Camacho,* &c.
Schumann (1810—1856),	*Geneviève.*
Flotow (*b.* 1811),	*Marta.*
Wagner (*b.* 1813),	*Tannhäuser, Lohengrin, Nibelungen.*
Wallace (1814—1865),	*Maritana, Lurline.*
Verdi (*b.* 1814),	*Il Trovatore, Rigoletto, Aïda.*
Gounod (*b.* 1818),	*Faust, Romeo et Juliet.*
Ambroise Thomas	*Mignon, Hamlet.*
Offenbach	*Orphée aux Enfers,* &c.

26. The following brief chronological summary of the rise and progress of Opera will further assist the student :—

Society of *Literati* established in Florence for the purpose of reviewing " the ancient Greek art of musical and dramatic declamation" (*musica parlante*)   ...   . (*c.*) 1580

First opera, *Dafne,* by Peri, libretto by Rinuceini ...   1594

Euridice, by Peri and Caccini   1600

Monteverde gives a more pronounced form to the Opera, and produces *Orfeo,* &c.   ...   ... (*c.*) 1650

Introduction of the Opera into Germany—Schütz' *Daphne*   1627

First performance of Spohr's *Faust*, at Prague ...	1816
Weber's *Der Freischütz* and *Preciosa* produced ...	1820
[Weber is supposed to have set the fashion of incorporating principal airs of the opera in the overture.]	
Meyerbeer's *Les Huguenots* produced	1836
Wagner's *Nibelungen* (Tetralogy) produced at a public festival in Bayreuth, Germany ...	1876

27. We have hitherto restricted our attention to the development of vocal music, accompanied or unaccompanied. We now turn to the consideration of purely **Instrumental Music**, a very wide branch of our subject, as it ranges from the pianoforte *morceau* to the elaborated symphony—from the "solo instrument" to the "full orchestra." The independent employment of instrumental music dates from a very early period. The Egyptian monuments show that bands of harps and other instruments existed in almost pre-historic times; certainly we can form no idea of the style or effect of the concerted music produced by these ancient minstrels. In the latter days of the old Grecian empire there sprang up a race of flute-players, but we are equally ignorant as to the nature of their performances. In the earlier ages of the Christian era instruments were generally used as an accompaniment to the voice; in fact the history of modern instrumental music as a distinct art, and as we now understand it, does not commence until about the sixteenth century. It is true that Royalty had its private bands as well as its vocalists, at a much earlier date, but if we except the startling "pibroch" of the Scottish bagpipes, the precise nature of the music performed is practically lost to us. Probably the *repertoire* of these old bands— such as the band of *weyghtes* or hautboys employed by Edward III. of England—consisted only of dance-tunes and the well-worn airs of popular songs. Nevertheless these ancient dance-tunes may be regarded as supplying the germs of some of the most elaborated forms of modern composition. The *coranto*, the *gavotte*, the

gigue, the *sarabande*, the *allemande*, the *galliard*, were all ancient dances, afterwards made " classical " by the studies of Corelli, Bach, Purcell, and other illustrious composers of the seventeenth and eighteenth centuries. The *suites-des-pièces* of these writers consisted of sets of three, four, or even a greater number of movements modelled upon these old dance-forms, and grouped together with a due regard to contrast between the pace or measure of each kind of dance. The following short extracts, taken from various sources,* will give the reader some idea of the principal dance-forms utilized in these *suites*:—

Ex. 26. Coranto. (*Lively.*)   Whitelocke.

&c.

Ex. 27. Allemande. (*Slow.*)   Dumont.

---

* We should make special acknowledgment of the following : Hawkins' *History of Music ;* Stainer and Barrett's *Dictionary of Musical Terms.*

Ex. 28. GAVOTTE.   *From the suite (for Orchestra) in D.*   J. S. BACH.

Allegro. f

&c.

Ex. 29. GALLIARD. *(Lively.)*   FRESCOBALDI.

&c.

Ex. 30. GIGUE or JIG. (*Lively.*) ECCLES.

&c.

Ex. 31. SARABANDE. (*Slow and stately.*) PURCELL.

&c.

Other dances were the *Bourrée, Carillon, Chaconne, Cotillon, Minuet, Passepied* (a variety of the minuet), *Polacca, Pavaine, Passecaille, Musette, Tarentelle, Hornpipe* (a species of gigue), *Rigadoon,* &c. Most of these dances were in use in the times of Elizabeth and Louis XIV., while the minuet and the gavotte remained fashionable at Court for a long time afterwards. The *suites* were written principally for the harpsichord, but also for strings, and for the organ. Many *suites* were arranged for violins and harpsichord, with a *basso continuo*, or figured bass for the latter. Among the most distinguished writers of *suites* are Corelli, Bach, Purcell, Handel, Couperin, Kühnau, Domenico Scarlatti, Alberti, &c.

28. Lutes and viols (of which more hereafter) were long employed only as accompaniments to the voice. Hawkins writes : " Concerning compositions of many parts adapted to viols, of which there are many, it is to be observed, that when the practice of singing madrigals began to decline, and gentlemen and others began to excel in their performance on the viol, the musicians of the time conceived the thought of substituting instrumental music in the place of vocal ; and for this purpose some of the most excellent masters of that instrument, namely Dowland, the younger Ferabosco, Coperario, Jenkins, Dr. Wilson, and many others, betook themselves to the framing compositions called Fantazias, which were generally in six parts, answering to the number of viols in a set or chest, ... and abounded in fugues, little responsive passages, and all those other elegancies observable in the structure and contrivance of the madrigal." As we have seen, viols were afterwards employed in *suites-des-piéces*.

29. It is to the *suite* that we owe the **Sonata**, justly regarded as one of the highest forms of composition. The primitive sonata, however, is scarcely to be identified with the class of composition now bearing that name. Those of Frescobaldi and others of this time are mostly single movements, and are sometimes called *Canzone.* In Purcell's time the sonata generally consisted of three or more movements ; the celebrated *Golden Sonata,* for two violins and a figured bass (by Purcell), is in five movements—*Largo, Adagio, Canzona* * *Allegro, Grave,* and *Allegro,* all (except the fourth

---

* The term *Canzona* is to be noted here.

movement, which is in the relative minor) being in the
key of F. The *Sonata di Chiesa*, belonging to about
the same period, consisted, as the name implies (*Church
Sonata*), of slow and solemn movements, mostly adapted
to the organ, while the secular and more lively composition was denominated *Sonata di Camera* (*Chamber
Sonata*). The movements usual in the modern Sonata
are, 1. The *Allegro*. This is the most important of all
as to its form, which is of the kind commonly called
Sonata, or more correctly, Binary ; *i. e.* it consists of
two subjects or themes, the first in the tonic, the
second in the dominant,—or relative major if the first
theme be in a minor key,—and the development and
recurrence of these two themes are to a great extent
guided by established rules, though much is left to the
individual skill and style of the composer. The
modern binary form was developed by Haydn ; after
him came Mozart ; while Beethoven perfected it in his
well-known sonatas and symphonies. 2. The *Andante*
or *Adagio*. This movement, usually with one principal
theme, *cantabile*, is generally in a related key other than
that of the dominant ; *e. g.* if the first movement be
written in the key of C, the *Andante* may be in F.
3. The *Minuet* or *Scherzo*. The latter, a more vigorous
movement than the Minuet, was introduced by Beethoven. 4. *Allegro* or *Presto*. This is written in the
original key (the same as that of the first movement)
and is generally of a freer character—the Rondo form,
consisting of only one principal theme of somewhat
frequent recurrence. But the forms of these after-
movements are not so essential to the sonata as that of
the first. In some compositions the second and last
movements will be found to be written in strict binary
form ; while in others even the first movement will be
found wanting in the essentials of the "sonata" proper.
Thus, the first movement of Beethoven's popular
"Sonata in A flat" (*Op.* 26) is nothing more than an
"air with variations·" while the sonatas of Schubert are

particularly erratic as to form. Sonatas have been written for the violin, the organ, the harpsichord or pianoforte, and for other instruments ; the following are the names of the principal composers who have written for the harpsichord, and later on for the pianoforte :—

Suites and (Early) Sonatas for Harpsichord.

Graziani (1609—1672).
Cesti (1624—1675).
Lully (1634—1687).
Biber (1648—1698).
Corelli (1653—1713).
Purcell (1658—1695).
A. Scarlatti (1659—1725).
Kühnau (1667—1722).
Buouoncini (1672—1750).
Albinoni (1674—1745).
Mattheson (1681—1722).
D. Scarlatti (1683—1757).
Durante (1684—1755).
J. S. Bach (1685—1750).
Handel (1685—1750).
Alberti (1705—1745).
Boyce (1710—1779).
W. F. Bach (1710—1784).
C. P. E. Bach (1711—1788).
Schobert (*c.* 1750).

Modern Sonatas for the Pianoforte.

Haydn (1732—1809).
Clementi (1752—1832).
Mozart (1756—1791).
Pleyel (1757—1831).
Dussek (1761—1812).
Steibelt (1764—1823).
Beethoven 1770—1827).
Cramer (1771—1858).
Hummel (1778—1837).
Field (1782—1837).
Ferd. Ries (1784—1838).
Kalkbrenner (1784—1849).

Modern Sonatas for the Pianoforte.

Onslow (1784—1853).
Weber (1786—1826).
Czerny (1794—1868).
Moscheles (1794—1870).
Schubert (1797—1828).
Schumann (1810—1856).
Mendelssohn (1809—1847).
Chopin (1810—1849).
Henselt (*b.* 1814).
Sterndale Bennett (1816—1875).

It should be added that the above composers were
more or less distinguished as performers on the harpsichord or pianoforte.

30. The *Sonata di Camera* has already been mentioned; the class "Chamber Music" (*Musica di Camera*)
includes many varieties of composition—all music, in
fact, which is capable of performance by a few persons.
Songs, glees, pianoforte solos or duets, and other
instrumental solos with or without pianoforte accompaniment, would properly come within the category.
But the term "Chamber Music" is now commonly
used to indicate works written for two or more instrumental performers, of whom there should be only *one* to
each part or instrument. Stringed, wood, and even
brass instruments of a not too noisy character, have
been employed in this species of music. Each performer being a soloist, especial care is taken with each
part, so that the skill of the player and the characteristic qualities of his instrument may be suitably
displayed. The earliest instrumental chamber music of
which anything certain is known was that composed
for the "sets of viols," and to which we alluded in
par. 27. The "fantasias" of Dowland, Jenkins, and
others of that date were generally written in six parts,
for the six instruments comprising a "chest of viols."
The modern compositions of this class, from the duet
to the octet, are usually written in the "sonata" form

described above, and may be familiarly described as sonatas for several instruments in concert, with this distinction, that each part is an individual voice ; not a mere contributary to complete harmony. Sammartini (1700—1775), Haydn, Boccherini, Mozart, Viotti, Pleyel, Shield (1754—1829), Grétry, Cherubini, Dussek, B. Romberg, Beethoven, Reicha, Georges Onslow, Hummel, Neukomm, Spohr, Ferdinand Ries, Weber, Fesca, Schneider, Schubert, Mayseder, Hauptmann, Molique, Reissiger, Mendelssohn, Schumann, Bennett, are among the most distinguished composers of chamber-music of the approved type.

31. The history of the **Concerto** may almost be said to run side by side with that of the *Musica di camera*, and may be regarded as forming the link between the latter and the purely orchestral *symphony*. The modern concerto is a composition for one principal instrument and the full orchestra, but the orchestra, although it cannot be regarded in the light of a mere accompaniment, is entirely subservient to the solo instrument, only coming in *fortissimo* when the soloist is in rest.* The most usual concertos are those for the pianoforte, or the violin ; but compositions of this kind have been written for the organ (by Handel, &c.), and for almost every orchestral instrument of importance—such as the flute (by Kühlau), the clarinet (by Weber), and the violoncello (by B. Romberg). The musical form of the earlier concertos by Corelli and others prior to, or contemporary with, Bach, was very similar to that of the "sonata" of the same period ; the present form is like that of the symphony, except that the concerto has fewer movements. The *minuet* is seldom, if ever, introduced in the modern concerto. We append a list of the principal composers of concertos.

---

* There are, of course, occasional exceptions to this rule, especially when the organ, or the pianoforte, is the solo instrument.

For the violin: Corelli, Tartini (1692—1770), Nardini, Lolli (1730—1802), Viotti (1753—1824), Baillot (1771—1842), Beethoven, Paganini (1784—1840), Spohr, De Beriot (1802—1870), Mendelssohn, &c.

For the pianoforte (or harpsichord) : J. S. Bach, Handel. Hasse, Sammartini, Friedemann Bach, C. P. E. Bach, J. C. Bach (the foregoing all for the harpsichord), Haydn, Boccherini, Grétry, Dittersdorf, Naumann, Clementi, Mozart, Pleyel, Dussek, Steibelt, Cramer, Beethoven, Weber, and others whose names have been mentioned as composers of pianoforte sonatas.

32. The term **Symphony** has been, and is still, so variously applied as to cause some confusion to young students. The introduction of a few bars usually written in songs is generally so called, while Handel and other composers of that time have inserted in their oratorios or cantatas short *intermezze* for the orchestra under the same name.* But the symphony proper, in the sense in which it is mentioned throughout this work, is a lengthy and highly elaborated composition for the full orchestra. The construction of the symphony is very similar to that of the pianoforte-sonata, both as regards the employment of the "binary" form and the number and style of the contrasting movements ; the only difference being—if difference it can be called—that the movements are more extended than in the ordinary sonata. The symphony is the highest form of orchestral work, and any number of instruments of the same and of various kinds may be employed, while solos for any players can be freely introduced. Beethoven has added voices to one of his symphonies—the ninth, commonly called the *Choral Symphony.* We have already said that any kind of instrument may be employed in the symphony ; but the following may be regarded as a fair specimen of the usual score :—

---

* *e. g.* the *Pastoral Symphony* in the *Messiah.*

1. Flutes,   *generally two* parts written.
2. Hautboys, *generally two*   „   „
3. Clarionets, *generally two*   „   „
4. Bassoons, *generally two*   „   „
5. Horns,   *two to four*   „   „
6. Trumpets, *generally two*   „   „
7. Trombones, *two or three*   „   „
8. Kettle Drums, *generally two, tuned in* 4^{ths} *or* 5^{ths}.
9. First Violins, *several instruments to one part.*
10. Second Violins,   „   „   „
11. Violas (or Tenors)   „   „
12. Violoncelli,   „   „   „
13. Double Basses,   „   „   „

Boccherini was one of the first to write symphonies
in correct form, but Haydn is really the founder of the
symphonic form as we have it to-day. Mozart elaborated it, Beethoven perfected it. Although many since
Beethoven have produced symphonies, some of them
really fine works, it cannot be said that any advance
either in form or orchestral effect has been made within
the last 50 years. Some of the later writers have
written a species of shortened symphony, called the
concert-overture; this is of about the same length as
the opera-overture, but more strict as to form. Overtures to well-known operas have always been popular
in the concert-room, and the concert-overture is a
result of this popularity. Schumann, Mendelssohn,
and Bennett; Brahms, and many other living composers, have written this class of orchestral work, which
is more modern than the symphony. The following
list includes as many writers of symphonies as the
student need remember :—

Hasse (1699—1783).
Sammartini (1700—1775).
Haydn (1732—1809), *London Symphonies, Toy Symphonies,*
    &c., 118 in all.
Gossec (1734 *—1829), *Symphonie en Re* (D).

---

* Schlüter erroneously gives the year 1773. Gossec died in his
ninety-sixth year.

Boccherini (1740—1806).
Naumann (1741—1801).
Grétry (1741—1813).
Clementi (1752—1832).
Mozart (1756—1791), *Jupiter Symphony,* and many others.
Pleyel (1757—1831), 29 symphonies.
A. Romberg (1769—1821).
Beethoven (1770 –1827), nine symphonies (*Pastorale, Eroica, Choral,* &c.).
Reicha (1770—1836).
Neukomm (1778—1858).
Onslow (1784—1852).
Spohr (1784—1859), *Die Weihe der Töne* (*The Power of Sound*), &c.
Moscheles (1794—1870).
Schubert (1797–1828), *Symphony in C,* &c.
Berlioz (1803—1869), *Romeo et Juliette,* &c.
Mendelssohn (1809—1847), *Scotch, Reformation,* and other symphonies.
Schumann (1810—1856), *Symphonies in C, B flat,* &c.
Liszt (*b.* 1811), *Faust Symphony, Tasso,* &c.
Bennett (1816—1875), *Symphony in C minor,* &c.
Niels Gade (*b.* 1817).

Amongst other symphonists now living may be mentioned J. Raff, Brahms, Joachim, Rubinstein, Sullivan, Prout, and Silas.

33. Having enumerated the principal forms of instrumental music, it now behoves us to give some account of the ancient and modern musical instruments ; we shall, however, confine our attention to those of especial note. Luscinius, in his *Musurgia* (1536), enters into many particulars concerning obsolete instruments, of some of which he supplies excellent wood-cuts : many of these are included in Hawkins' *History of Music,* and to this work we must refer those of our readers who are curious upon the subject. The more interesting among them shall be alluded to in the course of the present section.

34. The precise origin of the **Lyre** (λύρα), one of the most ancient of musical instruments, is wrapped in

obscurity, unless its invention is to be assigned to
Jubal, "the father of all that handle the 'harp' and
the organ." The lyre is undoubtedly of Asiatic origin,
was imported into Egypt, and thence into Greece. It
is a stringed instrument, of a size to be held by one
hand against the shoulder, while the other hand pulls
or "plucks" the strings. It has no neck or frets,
consequently the pitch of the strings cannot be altered
in playing, as with the "kithara" or guitar genus, to
which we shall refer by and bye. The lyre may in
fact be regarded as the prototype of the harp, and
secondarily of the harpsichord—from which last we
immediately derive the pianoforte. Into the old
traditions of the Greeks, who attribute the invention of
the lyre to Mercury, we shall not enter. Originally
the Greek lyre had but four strings; these were in-
creased by Terpander to seven; while later musicians
extended the number to eight, ten, fifteen, and, lastly,
even to sixteen strings. These strings were attuned to
the several Greek modes, and were plucked with the
fingers,* as an accompaniment to the voice.

35. The **Harp**, which stands next in relation to the
lyre, is one of the most ancient and universal of stringed
instruments, and has generally possessed a greater
number of strings and consequently a larger compass
than the lyre. The shape of the modern harp must be
familiar to every reader, and its triangular form is
almost identical with that of the Egyptian and Assyrian
harps as depicted on the ancient monuments. The
further we go back, however, we shall find these instruments more and more bow-like in shape; so that
there is good reason to believe that the first idea of the
harp was derived from the bow of the archer, the

---

* Instead of the fingers, a little stick or staff, made of bone,
metal, or a quill, and called a *plectrum* ($\pi\lambda\tilde{\eta}\kappa\tau\rho\upsilon$), was frequently
used for this purpose: hence the lyre, kithara, harp, lute, &c., are
known as "*plectral* instruments."

twang of the tightened string or cat-gut when plucked
giving forth a more or less definite tone or note.   In
Wales the harp is still regarded as the national instrument, as it has been from the earliest times; it is said,
however, that the Irish harp is even more ancient, that,
in fact, the Britons acquired it from the Irish Celts.
The harp has been tuned in various ways, sometimes
with a double row of strings (double harp or *Arpa
doppia*) proceeding by semitones; and the *triple* harp
—that is, having *three* rows of strings, is otherwise
known as the "Welsh harp." The harp has long been
recognized by composers as a valuable instrument in
the orchestra.   The *Arpa doppia*, or double harp,
already mentioned, was employed by Monteverde in
his opera *Orfeo*.   In Handel's *Saul* the harp is used as
a solo instrument, though the movements written for
it are not of a very distinctive character, and might
have been played with a similar effect upon the harpsichord.   In the scores of several modern operas the harp
has been introduced with splendid effect, and Wagner
has employed several of these instruments together.
The invention of the pedal action has by some been
attributed to Hochbrucker, 1720; by others to Velter,
1730.   This renders it possible that the pedal harp
was used in *Saul*, which was composed in 1738-9.   In
Esther, which was produced in 1720, the old Welsh
harp was employed.   About a century later (1820)
Erard introduced the *double* action, by which means
the strings may be raised two semitones, thus affording
greater facility for modulation.   The older, or *single-
action* harp, had seven pedals, raising the notes respectively affected one semitone only; the usual compass
of this instrument was nearly six octaves, its normal
scale being that of E flat.

   36. The **Spinet** (or Spinnet), sometimes called "the
Couched Harp," was a keyed instrument, and was the
prototype of the harpsichord. By some writers it is
mentioned as identical with the **Virginals**, described

by Luscinius in his *Musurgia* (1536). Certain it is that the action, compass, and shape of the instruments were very similar, if not identical. Either instrument had a single string for each note, which was sounded by the plectral action of a quill and jack set in motion by the key. The compass varied between three and four octaves, commencing from C or F below the bass stave. The smaller instruments were generally placed upon a table while being played upon. We have before alluded to the "Virginals" as the favourite musical instrument of Queen Elizabeth, for whom Dr. Tye composed many little "pieces" or studies. Byrde also wrote several compositions for the Virginals, which were printed in the collection known as Queen Elizabeth's Virginal Book.

37. The **Harpsichord** (Harpsicon, Clavicembalo, Clavecin, Cembalo), introduced into this country about the beginning of the seventeenth century, was an enlargement upon the spinet, both as regards power and compass. The notes were produced by the same action as that of the spinet, but in the harpsichord there were two, sometimes three, and even four brass or steel wires to each note, and "stops" were provided, by means of which the tone power could be intensified or diminished at the will of the player. Many instruments had a contrivance for the gradual opening and shutting of the lid, which gave the effect of a swell. Some had, besides, an upper keyboard, with a separate set of single strings which gave an effect similar to that produced by the soft pedal of the modern pianoforte. The usual compass of the harpsichord was five octaves, starting from the lowest bass note F :—

During the latter part of the seventeenth, and the greater portion of the eighteenth centuries, almost every orchestra contained the harpsichord, which occupied an important place in the scores, and was generally played by the conductor. The names of the more distinguished harpsichord players will be found included in the list of composers for that instrument given in paragraph 28 of the present section. A perusal of the harpsichord music of the Bachs and their contemporaries will show that, especially regarding the peculiar action of the instrument, the performers of that time were possessed of a wonderful degree of manipulative skill, some of their compositions being of a character to tax the executive powers of many of the best pianists of our own day. Until the middle of the last century the use of the thumb in playing was not allowed; it was Emmanuel Bach who, in 1753, first introduced a system of "fingering" in which the thumb was admitted. But no method of fingering, nor mechanical contrivance, could make the harpsichord a perfect instrument; it lacked, from the nature of its action, the capacity for producing that subtle, ever-varying "light and shade" which constitutes what is known as "expression."

38. It was the **Pianoforte** (Hammer-clavier) which, possessing the vital power of "expression," eventually superseded the harpsichord. The harp-like shape and the metal wires remained as in the older instrument, but the quills and jacks were displaced by the little hammers with which every one is familiar. Every degree of *piano* and *forte* being thus producible by the touch of the performer, the new instrument obtained its present name by common consent, as indicating a feature hitherto unknown in connection with keyed instruments. The idea of the pianoforte seems to have occurred coincidently to several persons about the same date; the earliest amongst them, however, appears to have been Cristofali, in 1711. The other co-inventors were Marius, Wood, and Schröter. The first noted

maker of pianofortes was Silbermann, whose instruments were much approved by Bach. This great musician does not appear, however, to have discarded the harpsichord in favour of the new instrument. It was not until 1760, ten years after the death of Bach, that the pianoforte came into popular favour. The earliest makers were Stein, Broadwood, Collard, Erard, and others whose names are well known at the present day in connection with pianoforte manufacture. Under the heads "Sonata" and "Concerto" we have mentioned the names of the principal composers for the pianoforte; the same musicians were celebrated likewise as *virtuosi*, or performers upon this instrument. We should, however, add to that list the following artists, who made pianoforte playing their special vocation: Herz, Thalberg, Schuloff; and amongst living celebrities, Hallé, Clara Schumann, Arabella Goddard, Liszt,* Rubinstein,* Von Bülow, Essipoff, Pauer.

39. The **Lute**, now obsolete, may be regarded as the most important of the many varieties of the *kithara* † genus. The period of the invention of the lute is still a matter of speculation; some say that it is of Asiatic origin. Dante (*d.* 1321) alludes to it in a manner which proves that it was a well-known instrument in his time. Mersennus (*d.* 1640) tells us that the lute consisted of three parts :—first, the table or flat soundboard lying under the lower end of the strings; secondly, the back or body, formed by nine convex ribs jointed together; thirdly, the neck, and in front of it the finger-board, over which nine frets or lines of cat-gut were stretched. The usual number of the strings was six, the five largest being doubled, making eleven strings in all. Many of the later instruments, however,

---

* *Vide* i. 68, 69.

† The *kithara* was distinguished from the *lyre* in the addition of a neck with frets lying close under the strings, by which means the pitch of each string could be raised by the "stopping" or pressure of the fingers.

had as many as twenty-four strings.   The lute was
usually tuned as under :

with two strings to each note, the highest excepted.
The *Orpharion-lute* had from sixteen to twenty strings,
which were of metal instead of cat-gut.   The Bass-lute
(*Theorbo*, Arch-lute, *Kithara bijuga*) had, as the last
name implies, two necks, or, more correctly, two heads
and fret-boards of different sizes and placed side by
side,—the longer fret-board for the bass strings, and the
shorter for the upper and middle strings.   The theorbo
came into use about the beginning of the seventeenth
century, and formed a valuable constituent in the early
orchestra.   Thomas Mace, in his quaintly-written
treatise, *Musick's Monument* (1676), has given an
interesting description of the theorbo, for which he
was a very popular composer.   Music for the lute was
written in a peculiar kind of notation, called *tablature*,
consisting of letters and other signs upon a six-line
stave.   Performers on the lute or theorbo were termed
"lutenists," and until recent years existed the office
of "Lutenist in the Chapel Royal."   The theorbo fell
into disuse about the middle of the last century.   Some
writers affirm that the latest employment of this instrument in the orchestra was by Francesco Conti, in 1708,
but this statement is not correct.   Handel used it in
his *Ode on Saint Cecilia's Day*, which was composed
and produced in 1739, as an accompaniment to the air
"The Soft Complaining Flute."   The score is marked
"Liuta," but the compass employed

conclusively indicates the theorbo.   In old scores we frequently find the part for the theorbo written as a *basso continuo*, or figured bass.   Among the most eminent lutenists were Mace, Kapsberger, Lambert, Conti, Gaetano, and Gauthier.   Hawkins gives the following specimen of lute music, composed by Thomas Mace :

Ex. 32. MY MISTRESS.   THOMAS MACE.

Other varieties of the *kithara* family were the glittern or cither, the citole, the mandolin (employed by Mozart in *Don Giovanni*), and the guitar, which has enjoyed a more recent popularity.   The hackbret or dulcimer may scarcely be said to belong to the same order, as its strings were not "plucked," but beaten by small pellets or hammers, upon the principle of the modern pianoforte.

40. The family of stringed instruments played with a bow has been a very numerous one.   The most ancient viol on record appears to be the *ravenstrom* (or ravanastron), still played in India by the mendicant monks of Buddha.   Tradition says that this primitive instrument was invented by one of the kings of Ceylon, but as the date assigned to this monarch is somewhere about five thousand years before Christ, the tradition is worth very little indeed.   It is said, however, that the ravenstrom was the precursor of the *youdok*, or

Russian fiddle ; and the Welsh *crwth*, which had six strings strung across a flat bridge, and was played partly with the bow, and partly by plucking with the fingers. Another ancient variety is the *urh-heen* of the Chinese, which consists of a mallet-shaped box, into which a stick or tube is fixed, with three or four strings strung from pegs at one end of the stick and passing over a bridge fixed upon the mallet-like box. The *trumpet-marine* consisted of a triangular box with one string strung across a very low bridge. From the *rebab* of Egypt, a single-stringed fiddle with a square-shaped body, is probably derived the *rebec*, a three-stringed instrument in shape more nearly resembling the modern violin. From the *rebec* sprang in fact the family of viols to which frequent allusion has been made. The *Viol*, or *vitula*, dates from the tenth or eleventh century ; it usually had six strings, and the finger-board was furnished with frets. The size of the viol was approximate to that of the viola, or tenor violin now used in the orchestra. The " chest of viols " has been described by an old writer as " a large hutch with several apartments and partitions in it, each lined with green baize. Every instrument was sized in bigness according to the part played upon it, the treble being the smallest," &c. A model chest of viols contained six instruments,—two trebles, two tenors, and two basses. From the chest of viols we obtain the **Violoncello**; also the *Viol-da-gamba*, or leg-viol, so called from the position in which it is held by the performer. The finger-board of the *gamba* was provided with frets, and the strings, six in number, were thus tuned :

The viol-da-gamba was an instrument much favoured by Bach, who wrote *obbligati* parts for it in some of his scores—one notable instance occurs in the *Passion according to St. Matthew.* Bach invented a similar instrument, having a somewhat higher compass, which he named *Viola pomposa,* but this was soon superseded by the violoncello. The *Baryton,* or *Viol-di-Bardone,* was another instrument of the viol class, having six to seven cat-gut strings played with the bow, under which lay sixteen metal strings which were plucked with the fingers of the left hand. Prince Esterhazy, the patron of Haydn, was exceedingly fond of this instrument, for which Haydn composed upwards of one hundred and sixty studies. A very similar instrument, both as to the number of cat-gut strings and the metal strings beneath, was the *Viol-d'amour,* which Meyerbeer has employed for a special effect in *Les Huguenots.* The **Double bass** (*contra-basso*), the largest of all the viols, is said to have been invented by Salo, in 1580; Monteclair introduced it into the orchestra in 1696.

41. The actual inventor of the **Violin**, or little viol, is not known, nor yet the precise date of its introduction. The earliest mention of the instrument as a constituent of the orchestra seems to be that given by Monteverde in the list of the orchestra at the performance of his *Orfeo,* 1650 :—" *Duoi violini piccoli alla Francese ;* "— two little violins of the French sort. But that at this date the violin was not a novelty is patent from the fact that the violin manufacture was commenced by the elder AMATI about the year 1600. We further hear of oné BALTAZARINI giving violin performances in England in 1577. From the recent research of a German antiquarian it seems tolerably conclusive that the violin manufacture was initiated in Germany, and was imported thence into Italy. The principal Italian makers of the seventeenth century were the AMATI, the GUARNERI, and the STRADIUARI families (all of Cremona), who so jealously guarded the peculiar secrets of their manufacture, that no modern maker has so far been able to reproduce instruments of the same quality.

Others of the same period were JACOBUS STAINER or STEINER, ALBANUS, and the KLOTZ family—these were the principal German makers. The following distinguished violinists are named in approximate chronological order : BALTAZARINI, LULLY, BALTZAR, BANISTER, BASSANI, CORELLI, TARTINI, LOCATELLI, JARNOVICK, BITTI, ALBINONI, GIARDINI, CAMPAGNOLI, LUNATI, DIEUPART, PERGOLESI, LE CLAIR, GEMINIANI, LOLLI, VIOTTI, BAILLOT, KREUTZER, RODE, MAYSEDER, PAGANINI, LAFONT, SPOHR, DE BERIOT. The principal violinists of the present day it is unnecessary to mention.

42. Among WIND INSTRUMENTS, probably the most ancient is the **Flute**, of which there have been many varieties. The word "flute" is supposed to be derived from *fluta*, a lamprey, or small eel, which has on its side seven marks or holes corresponding to those of the instrument. The flute was exceedingly popular with both the Greeks and the Romans, who introduced flute playing into their religious ceremonies, and almost on every public occasion—indeed, even at their funerals. At first, and until a comparatively recent date, the mouth-piece and shape of the flute was not unlike the flageolet. Some flutes were " double," *i.e.*, having two tubes connected with a single mouth-piece. Luscinius describes flutes of four sizes, ranging from treble to bass. The *Recorder,* frequently alluded to by the old English writers, was a kind of flageolet, and varied in length from about twelve inches to three feet, the largest being the *Bass Recorder.* The *Pilgrim's Staff* was the name given to one kind of flute from its great length and consequent resemblance to the staves carried by religious pilgrims in their processions. The *Cornet,* not to be confounded with the modern brass instrument of the same name, was a bow-shaped flute, tapering towards the mouth-piece, and came into use in the reign of Elizabeth. The tone of the cornet was regarded as very closely resembling the human voice, and for this reason, at the Restoration, when Cathedral

choristers were yet very scarce, owing to the discouragement of choral services by the Puritans, this instrument was used to strengthen the treble parts. The old English flute, or *flute-à-bec*,—so called because the mouthpiece had some resemblance to the bill or "beak" of a bird,—was the flute commonly used in the orchestra up to the time of Handel, who introduces into some of his scores the modern horizontal or German flute (*flauto traverso*), as the *traverso*, evidently to distinguish it from the *flute-à-bec*, still in general use in his day.

43. Of the present REED INSTRUMENTS the **Oboe** (or *hautboy*) is one of the oldest. Its use in England may be traced as far back as the fourteenth century. They were employed in the court band of Edward III., and were then known as *weyghtes* or *waites ;* and it is further supposed that the Christmas "waits" derived their appellation from the fact that these *waites* or hautboys were a prominent feature of those nocturnal entertainments. In the plays of Shakespeare, we find frequent allusion to the "hautboys" in the stage directions announcing the entry of royal or martial pageants. The **Corno Inglese** (*Cor Anglais*) is, familiarly speaking, a larger oboe, and forms the "alto" of the smaller instrument. The *Orfeo* of Gluck contains a part for this instrument, as well as the overture in Rossini's *Guillaume Tell ;* while Meyerbeer has introduced it into many of his scores. The instrument has also been employed by Wagner and some other modern writers. The "natural bass" of the above instruments is the **Bassoon** (called in Italian *fagotto*, from its resemblance, when the parts are severed and tied together, to a bundle of sticks or faggots), said to have been invented in the year 1539 by an Italian named Afranio, but there is no doubt that it was of much earlier date, though of different shape and compass, and was known as the *Bombard*, or Bass *Weyghte*. It is not, however, to be confounded with the *Basaun* mentioned by Luscinius, which was really a bass

instrument of the trombone (or sackbut) class. Handel
was one of the first among important composers to
introduce the bassoon into the orchestra, and his use of
the instrument in *Saul* (in the Incantation scene,
Infernal Spirits, and *Why hast thou forced me?*) is
an instance well known to musicians. The same
master has employed the bassoon to great advantage in
Thou didst blow, in *Israel in Egypt.* Since Handel's
time the bassoon has taken an important place in the
orchestra. The *Double Bassoon*, the compass of which
is an octave below that of the bassoon, was first introduced into the orchestra at the Handel Commemoration
in Westminster Abbey, 1784. Owing to the unwieldy
size of the instrument it has been very sparingly
employed by musicians; nevertheless Beethoven has
introduced it in two of his symphonies—the C minor,
and the "Choral," with imposing effect.

44. The modern **Clarinet** was the invention of
Denner of Nuremberg, in 1690; some writers, however,
give the date as 1720. Its predecessor was the *Chalameau,** or *Schalmey*, sometimes mentioned as the
precursor of the oboe. The term "chalameau" is still
employed to denote the lower and middle registers of
the clarinet, which was first used in the orchestra about
the middle of the last century. It had a place in the
score of an opera, *Orione*, by J. C. Bach (a son of the
great master), composed about 1760. The alto and
bass clarinets are simply larger varieties of the smaller
instrument, each producing a correspondingly lower
compass. The **Basset-Horn** (*Corno di bassetto*), which
has been described as taking an intermediate place
between the clarinet and bassoon, is of comparatively
modern date, although seldom used in modern scores.
Lotz, of Presburg, in Germany, introduced it in 1782;
and Mozart appears to be the first master of note who
adopted it. His *Clemenza di Tito*, and more notably

* From *calamus*, a reed.

still, the *Requiem*, both contain remarkable illustrations of the striking properties, the individual excellencies of this much neglected instrument. The *Basset-Horn* resembles in shape a large clarinet, having a metal bell. The compass of the instrument ranges from the lower bass F to the middle C in the treble stave. The instrument might be considered obsolete but for its employment in military bands. The **Serpent**, which dates from 1590, scarcely belongs to the clariuet class, but it may be mentioned here in concluding our notice of wood instruments. The Serpent has a compass similar to that of the bassoon, but its alleged uncertainty of tone-production has long since brought it into disfavour, although we have heard it remarked by instrumentalists of experience, that in the hands of a skilful player it could still be made to form a most valuable addition to the orchestra of the present day.

45. We can only glance at the principal members of the numerous family of BRASS INSTRUMENTS. The **Horn** (*Corno*), though the least assertive among brass instruments, adds so greatly to the colouring of symphonic music, that it has always occupied an honoured place in the orchestra. It is also one of the most ancient of instruments, being at least of mediæval origin. The Horn for which Beethoven and other great masters wrote, is the primitive one called the French Horn, which simply produces the natural harmonics of the open tube, other notes, always sparingly used, being artificially formed by the insertion of the hand in the bell. In 1748, Hampel, a German, invented a plan for the production of the semitones; Kölbel, Müller, and others tried further improvements, but the later invention of Saxe (the use of pistons) completely overcame the mechanical difficulties, while at the same time the tone of the instrument deteriorated. The *Trumpet* (*Clarino, tromba*) is of equal antiquity with the horn, and its notes are similarly produced, but of higher pitch and more brilliant tone. The scores of the last

century show that the trumpets of that time were
capable of producing higher notes than at the present
day, the probability being that the instruments were
then altogether smaller in the tube and bell.* The
Trombone, formerly known as the *sackbut*, figured in
the scores of the sixteenth century.   G. Gabrieli (1540
—1612) employed four sackbuts in the accompaniments
to his *Surrexit Christus*, and at this the musician is
inclined to smile ; but it is not improbable that they
were used to double or lead the voice parts, each
represented by a goodly number of singers.   Again,
the trombone was included in the score of Monteverdi's
Orfeo.   The presence of the trombone in some of
Handel's scores has been ascribed to Mozart, but this is
now considered more than doubtful.   There are four
species or sizes of trombone, the soprano, the alto,
the tenor, and the bass.   The first and fourth kinds
are seldom now used ; the latter owing to its being
fatiguing to the performer, and of sluggish utterance.
Other bass instruments are the *Bombardon*, the *Tuba*,
the *Euphonium*, of comparatively recent date ; and the
Ophicleide, which was invented to supersede the serpent
in the orchestra.

46. It now remains to us to give a short summary of
the development of the **Organ**, the most comprehensive
of all instruments.   In histories of the organ it is
usual to give a description of a small collection of
pipes worked by hydraulic action, known as "the
water-organ of the ancients ;" but although diagrams
are supplied with the description, the account is somewhat apocryphal.   The *Magrepha*, or organ of ten
pipes, with a keyboard, is alleged to have existed in
the second century, but doubts have been expressed
regarding the nature of this instrument also.   It is,
however, an historical fact, that an organ, the gift of

---

* The *Claret*, *Felt*, and *Thürnerhorn*, mentioned by Luscinius,
were all ancient varieties of the Clarion or trumpet.

Constantine, was in the possession of King Pepin of France *circa* A.D. 757. Still earlier (*circa* 700), Aldhelm, a monk, makes mention of an organ with "gilt pipes," though he gives no clue to the size of the instrument. In the tenth century, an organ having 400 pipes is mentioned by Wolstan; the organ was played with "keys," and was blown by thirteen separate pairs of bellows. Drawings of this period still extant represent the organ as an instrument having but few pipes, blown with evident labour by two or more persons, and played upon by a monk. The keys of these organs were of wood, of from three to six inches in breadth, and requiring to be played upon by hard blows of the fist. Thus it is plain that these instruments were not capable of yielding more than the plain song or melody of ancient Church music, or at most, the crude *organum* or diaphony to which we have elsewhere alluded. The "half-notes," or semitones, were introduced at Venice about the end of the eleventh century; even at this date the compass of the instrument was limited to two octaves. The invention of the organ pedal is attributed to Bernhardt, * about 1490; and the compass was an octave from B flat or A. These pedals were nothing more than small pieces of wood of a size to be played with the toe—in fact, the heel was not used until a comparatively recent period. The "swell organ" was first introduced by Jordan in 1712; the Venetian swell, by which a more gradual *crescendo* and *diminuendo* is effected was the invention of England, towards the end of the last century. The swell was further improved by Green, a well-known organ-builder of the same period. As the organ developed, in the course of time, into the character of a solo instrument,† the ingenuity of musicians and organ-builders (who

† The *Regale*, or *Regals*, was a small portable organ (now obsolete), in use during the sixteenth and seventeenth centuries. This, probably, was the instrument which proved so great a solace to Milton in his blindness.　　　　* *Vide* i. 24.

were as great enthusiasts in their calling as the Italian
violin-makers were in theirs) was exercised in the
production of new varieties of tone and register. The
smaller wind-instruments were more or less successfully
imitated, and their names are still associated with
certain organ-stops—notably the *Krumhorne* (*Cremorne,
Cremona*), the *Gemshorn,* and the *Hohl flöte.* The
most celebrated builders in England during the last
century were Abraham Jordan, "Father" Schmidt,
Harris, Snetzler, Schröder, Avery, Byfield, and Green.
Organ-playing as a separate art undoubtedly owes much
to Frescobaldi, who has been called "The father of
organ-playing;" he wrote fugues and other compositions
in which he expressly studied the capicities of the
instrument of his day. The following list of celebrated
organists includes those chiefly who were reputed for
their special skill as performers, or composers of organ-
music. We have not thought it necessary to mention
living organists :—

> Dr. John Bull (1563—1622).
> Viadana (1560—1625).
> Frescobaldi (1580—1640).
> Gibbons (1583—1625).
> Kerl (1625—1690).
> Froberger (1637—1695).
> Buxtehude (*c.* 1640—1707).
> Stradella (1645—1678).
> Blow (1648—1708).
> Purcell (1658—1695).
> Couperin (1668—1733).
> Caldara (1678—1763).
> Mattheson (1681—1764).
> Walther (1683—1729).
> J. S. Bach (1685—1750).
> Handel (1685—1759).
> Hasse (1699—1783).
> Boyce (1710—1779).
> Marpurg (1719—1789).
> Albrechtsberger (1736—1809).
> Stadler (1748—1833).
> Vogler (1749—1818).

Rink (1770—1846).
Mendelssohn (1809—1847).
S. Sebastian Wesley (*d.* 1876).
George Cooper (*d.* 1876).

47. The foremost among INSTRUMENTS OF PERCUSSION is the **Drum** (*tambour*, tympanum), consisting of a hollow hemisphere or cylinder of wood or metal, over the mouth or ends of which is placed a skin or parchment, in tension. The pitch of the note produced may be raised or lowered by the tightening or slackening, as the case may be, of the parchment disc; this being effected by screws or bracings of leather working upon cords. The drum most commonly used in the orchestra is the hemispherical or "*kettle-drum*," generally a pair tuned at the distance of a fourth or fifth from each other—tonic and dominant. Beethoven has produced some remarkable effects from the drum—for example, the enharmonic change in the first movement of the fourth symphony (in B flat), when the original tonic (B flat) drum is unexpectedly employed as A$\sharp$. Berlioz, than whom no man better understood the resources of the orchestra, made a special study of the drum; and in his Requiem upon the death of Napoleon I. introduced several sets of kettle-drums *sordini*. The great or long drum (*bass drum*, *grosse caisse*) is very sparingly used by composers, who employ it only in *fortissimi* passages, such as in the chorus "*Come with torches*" in the *Walpurgis Night* of Mendelssohn. The *Glockenspiel* is a frame of bells—sometimes of steel bars, possessing a fair compass of simply diatonic intervals, and struck with hammers, with the hand, or by keys as in the pianoforte. Mozart uses a glockenspiel with exquisite effect in his *Zauberflöte*. The *Carillon* which Handel used in *Saul* was an instrument very similar to, if not identical with, the glockenspiel.

48. In the above review—necessarily cursory—of the principal musical instruments, past and present, we have mainly followed the plan adopted by Berlioz in

his Treatise on Instrumentation; and, like him, we have
reserved to the last our mention of that most exalted
of all "instruments of music," the HUMAN VOICE.
We have already, in our first section (i. 8, 9, 11, 12,
13, 29), alluded to the schools of singing founded by
Ambrose, Gregory, Charlemagne, and other early patrons
of music, or musicians, in connection with ecclesiastical
music.   Of the early institution of church choirs we
have already treated in the present section (par. 3),
and with the growth of the contrapuntal art may be
traced the development of choral harmony, with its
divisions of soprano, alto or contralto, tenor and bass.
With respect to solo-singing, we have to look to the
troubadours, the minnesänger, and other secular vocalists
for the birth of the present art, but more immediately to
the opera, which gave a new and larger scope for vocal
skill.   In the earlier days of the opera the female as
well as the male characters were acted by men (for a
long time women were not allowed upon the stage), to
which end, by an artificial process, the treble voice of
boyhood was preserved to them through life.   Among
such male *soprani* may be mentioned, Senesino,
Bernacchi, Caffarelli, Farinelli; in fact, male *soprani*
continued in favour with the public long after the
advent of female opera singers.   Of the latter, Hawkins
gives a long list, of which we may note the following:
San Nicola, Santini (afterwards the wife of Ant·nio
Lotti). Boschi, Mrs. Tofts, Maria Gallia (who took the
part of *Rosamund* in Clayton's opera of that name),
Margarita de l'Epine, Mrs. Barbier, Anastasia Robinson
(afterwards Countess of Peterborough), Faustina; other
celebrated female singers of the last century were Tesi,
Cuzzoni, Francesca Gabrieli, Mrs. Billington, &c.
Belonging to the present century were Catalani (*d.* 1849),
Sontag, Clara Novello, Pasta, Jenny Lind, Malibran,
Giulia and Giulietta Grisi, Mara, Alboni, Titiens (*d.*
1877), Patti, Nillson, Patey; some of whom are still
living, and some in retirement.   Among the tenor and

bass singers of the last fifty years are : Tamburini, Lablache, Staudigl, Wachtel, Rubini, Raff, Kelly, Mario, Braham, Sims Reeves, Santley, &c. Many of these artists distinguished themselves in oratorio as well as in opera.

49. The ancient schools of singing have been succeeded by *Conservatoires* or Academies, where every branch of the musical art is cultivated and taught. Amongst the Academies which possess an historic fame are the Conservatoires of Milan, Bologna, Berlin, Leipsic, Paris, and the Royal Academy of Music in London. The Royal Academy of Music, which was founded in 1822, and afterwards incorporated by Charter, has passed through many vicissitudes, but has succeeded in establishing for itself a position worthy of the English nation, and has given to the world many esteemed musicians, of whom the late Sterndale Bennett is a notable instance. Other institutions established for the promotion of musical learning are, the College of Organists, established in 1864, for the benefit of organists and other church musicians ; Trinity College, London, instituted in 1872, and afterwards incorporated by Charter, for the promotion of musical and general education ; the National Training School for Music, which commenced its useful work in 1876 ; the Royal Irish Academy of Music ; and other important institutions, all of which, in their several capacities and spheres of work, have combined to further the musical progress of this country. Nor can we omit a reference to the Tonic Sol-fa movement, which for several years has been spreading through our own and other English-speaking countries, and has undoubtedly done much to improve the musical knowledge and taste of the masses. In 1875, the leaders of the movement obtained a Charter for an institution which bears the name of the Tonic Sol-fa College, and many connexional choral bodies have been formed, and trained on the Tonic Sol-fa principles, the most important of which are the

syllabic notation and the " Moveable Do." It is not
within the province of this work to discuss the merits
or demerits of this system, about which there has been
much unprofitable controversy.

50. It now only remains to us to enumerate the
principal writers on the **Science** of music. The
voluminous Latin Treatise of BOËTHIUS (*d.* 525) was
based to a great extent upon the ancient dissertations
of Pythagoras, Aristoxenus, Ptolemy, and others, and
entered with great minuteness into the mathematical
ratios of intervals, dealing of course with the old Greek
scales. CASSIODORUS (*c.* 470—560), a distinguished
scholar of the same period, also wrote concerning the
science of music, but added little or nothing to the
extensive and somewhat mystic lore amassed by
Boëthius. Allusion has already been made to the
more practical treatises of Guido, Isidore of Seville,
and Franco of Cologne. Succeeding writers, such as
Odington, Tinctor, De Handlo, Gaffurius, Franchinus,
and others, founded their observations on the Boëthian
and Guidonian systems. The inauguration of the modern
science is due chiefly to *Dr. William Holder* (*d.* 1697)
and *Rameau* (1683 — 1764). Dr. Holder's treatise
on Harmony (1694) is worthy of note as containing
the scheme of natural harmonics, familiarized to us by
the later works of Logier and Ouseley. Hawkins thus
summarizes this portion of Dr. Holder's work : " He
makes a concord to consist in the coincidence of the
vibrations of the chords of two instruments, and speaks
to this purpose :—If the vibrations correspond in every
course and recourse, the concord produced will be the
unison ; if the ratio of the vibrations be as 2 to 1, in
which case they will unite alternately, viz , at every
course, crossing at the recourse, the concord will be the
octave. If the vibrations be in the ratio of 3 to 2,
their sounds will consort in a fifth, uniting after every
second, *i. e.*, at every other or third course ; and if as
4 to 3, in a diatessaron or fourth, uniting after every

third recourse, viz., at every fourth course, and so of
the other consonances according to their respective
ratios." On that part of the theory of music which
relates to the formation or derivation of chords there
have been many writers, but among these none has, we
imagine, been the cause of so much controversy among
musicians as the theories of Dr. Day, whose chief
exponent at the present time is Professor Macfarren.
To explain the respective doctrines held by Day,
Ouseley, and Stainer would need, to do justice to the
subject, a separate work ; here we can only assure the
young student that whatever differences may exist
among theorists as to the etymology of a chord (*e. g.*,
whether it has one root or two roots) the mode of its
employment and resolution are identical in every case
—that is, the practical effect is the same.   The harmony
treatises of Crotch, Catel, Callcott, and Goss, have dealt
almost exclusively with the practical side of the subject.
The works of the three former writers, however, are generally regarded as being "behind the times." Of Counterpoint and Fugue the most prominent expositors have
been : Zarlino (1517—1593), *Fux*, or Fuchs (1660—
1732), Padre Martini (1706—1784), *Marpurg* (1718—
1795), Albrechtsberger (1736—1809), *Cherubini* (1760
—1842), and Reicha (1770—1836).   Bach's *Art of
Fugue,* published in 1748, is simply a collection of fine
examples, all on one subject, of this form of composition.
Chief among the critics, historians, and miscellaneous
writers on musical science and art, during the past and
present centuries are : J. Mattheson (1681—1764), essayist and historian; J. J. Rousseau (1712—1778), essayist;
Sir John Hawkins (1720—1791), historian; Dr. Charles
Burney (1726—1814), historian ; O. F. Langlé (1741
—1807), theorist; Grétry (1741—1813), essayist;
J. N. Forkel (1749—1818), essayist and historian :
C. F. Zelter (1758—1832), essayist ; A. E. Choron
(1772—1834), theorist; Giuseppe Baini (1775—1844),
historian; F. J. Fétis (1784—1872), essayist and

historian; A. B. Marx (1799 — 1866), theorist; H. Berlioz (1803—1869), essayist; R. Schumann (1810—1856), essayist; also Ambros, Liszt, Engel, Rimbault, Chappell, Hullah, Ritter, &c., &c.

51. There is, however, another and a distinct class of musical philosophers, whom we may call the SCIENTISTS of the present day; men whose researches as physicists have led them into a special inquiry into the natural laws and phenomena of sound. To this class belong Wheatstone, Tyndal, Blaserna, and many others whose names must be familiar to every reader of contemporary musical literature. But undoubtedly the most distinguished amongst musical scientists is HELMHOLTZ, the German physicist and physician, whose work *Die Lehre von den Tonempfindungen*, recently translated into English by Mr. A. J. Ellis, has opened, as it were, a new world to the view of the musician. It may be said that the art of music profits little by these physical discoveries; but while the science is still in its infancy, we cannot predicate with certainty concerning the result of all this recent research. It may be that, at any moment, while the pen is in the hand, or the lips are moved to speech, some sudden burst of light, some new and splendid apocalypse, shall, by the instrumentality of science, irradiate the whole world of music, revealing forms of beauty, and spheres of vision, hitherto beclouded or unknown.

EXAMINATION QUESTIONS.*

SECTION I.

1 What do you know of the musical scales of the Greeks?
2 From whom did the Greeks derive the rudiments of their musical knowledge?
3 In what sense is the term "Harmony" employed by the Greek writers?
4 Who were the most noted among Greek Theorists?
5 Who introduced the art of flute-playing into Greece?
6 What ancient nation employed Greek slaves as singers and players?
7 When may the history of music as a separate art be said to commence?
8 About what date, and by whom, was the first singing school instituted in Rome?
9 Upon what evidence do we infer that St. Sylvester was acquainted with the method of antiphonal chanting?
10 When did St. Ambrose live; and what did he do for Church Music?
11 What were the "Authentic Modes?" The "Plagal Modes?" Give a list of them as arranged by St. Gregory.

---

* The Student is requested to search out for himself the answers to these questions, the numbers prefixed to them having (designedly) no reference to the body of the work.

12 What was meant by the term Diaphony? Organum?
13 Name some of the improvements effected by Guido
     in the old system of notation.
14 What title has been applied to Guido?
15 From what devices are our present C and F clefs
     derived?
16 When was the note *Si* introduced?
17 Who introduced the system of musical measure
     (*musica mensurabilis*)?
18 Give the names and shapes of the notes used by
     Franco.
19 What was the state of counterpoint in Franco's time?
20 Who was the inventor of " rest " signs?
21 Give some account of Adam de la Hale.
22 Name some of the most distinguished troubadours
     of De la Hale's time.
23 Who has been credited with having established the
     first correct principles of consonances and dis-
     sonances?
24 To whom is ascribed the introduction of florid
     counterpoint?
25 State what you know of Dufay, and of the rise of
     the Belgian School.
26 Which of the early Belgian composers has been
     styled "the Sebastian Bach of the fifteenth
     century," and on what grounds?
27 What is your impression concerning the character
     of the " fugues " composed by the early Belgian
     masters?
28 Des Prés effected an important advance in the art
     of musical composition. What was it?
29 Name some of the most distinguished pupils of Des
     Prés.
30 What was Luther's opinion of Des Prés' music?
31 A pupil of Des Prés has been styled " the founder
     of the Venetian School." Give his name.
32 To whom is ascribed the introduction of the
     Madrigal?

33 Who was the most distinguished contemporary of Willaert?

34 Who introduced the chromatic element into musical composition?

35 Who was the first to use the terms *Adagio, Allegro,* &c.?

36 What were the principal failings of the Belgian School?

37 When was the organ-pedal invented, and by whom?

38 Give the date of the invention of moveable music-types, and the name of the inventor.

39 Who has been called the "father of English contra-puntists?"

40 Who wrote the anthem, *I will exalt Thee, O Lord?*

41 What was Merbecke's principal work?

42 Give a short account of Thomas Tallis.

43 Which of the early English musicians wrote a motett in forty parts?

44 Give the name of a famous canon by William Byrde.

45 Who was the first professor of music at Gresham College?

46 What was "The Virginal Book?" for whom was it written?

47 Give the title of a celebrated collection of madrigals published about the beginning of the seventeenth century, and name some of the principal contributors to the work.

48 Who was Constanzo Festa? What is his place in the history of Church Music?

49 Name a distinguished pupil of Goudimel.

50 Give an account of the controversy which occasioned the production of *Missa Papae Marcelli.*

51 What was the name given to the style of composition of which *Missa Papae Marcelli* was the inauguration?

52 Who was Nanini?

53 A six-part motett, *Lamentabatur Jacobus,* composed
   by a Spaniard, is still performed in the Sistine
   Chapel at Rome.   Give the name of the composer.
54 In what style of composition did Marenzio particularly excel ?
55 Who introduced instrumental accompaniments in
   the music of the Church ?   Name the instruments
   employed by this composer.
56 Trace the origin of the Opera.
57 What was *musica parlante ?*
58 Give the name, date, and composer of the first
   Italian Opera.
59 On what special occasion was *Euridice* produced ?
60 To what great composer of the seventeenth century
   was it reserved to give a more pronounced form
   to the Opera ?
61 For what practices was Monteverde subjected to
   the unfavourable criticisms of his contemporaries ?
62 Name the principal Operas of Monteverde.
63 Give an account of the circumstances attending the
   rise of Oratorio.
64 Account for the term *Oratorio,* as applied to that
   class of composition.
65 What was the first oratorio produced, and who was
   the composer ?
66 Name some of the improvements effected in oratorio
   by Carissimi.
67 An oratorio by Carissimi has recently been revived.
   Give the title.
68 Which of the Italian composers is said to have
   written the first Church concertos and solo songs
   for the Church ?
69 Give the earliest known date of the employment of
   the *basso continuo,* or figured bass.
70 Name an accomplished Italian Organist of the
   seventeenth century.
71 Who was "the first to write harmony as distinguished from counterpoint ? "

72 Name the best-known composition of Allegri.
73 To whom is attributed the introduction of the Chorale ?
74 Who was the " father of German Oratorio ?"
75 Give the title of the first German Opera, the date of its production, and the name of the composer.
76 To what important musical post was Gibbons appointed ?
77 Name a well-known Anthem by Orlando Gibbons.
78 By what well-known composition is Matthew Lock chiefly remembered ? Is it universally admitted that Lock composed that work ?
79 Name " the greatest English musical genius."
80 Who was Henry Purcell's master ?
81 Enumerate the principal amongst Purcell's works.
82 Who was Dr. Aldrich ?
83 Name an anthem by Dr. Croft containing a six-part fugue.
84 Who composed the celebrated anthem, *Hear my crying ?*
85 Give a short account of Dr. Boyce, naming some of his principal works.
86 A contemporary of Boyce wrote as many as twenty-three operas. Give his name.
87 Name an anthem by Battishill, written for seven voices.
88 What German composer is supposed to form the link between Schütz and Bach ?
89 Who wrote *The Bleeding and dying Jesus ?* In what respect does the plan of this work differ from that of the Passion-music of Bach ?
90 Give an account of the career of Sebastian Bach.
91 How many Passion-oratorios did Bach write ?
92 What was the mode of performance originally intended for the *Christmas Oratorio ?*
93 Did Bach write any music for the Roman Church ?
94 Describe the *Suites Anglaises.*

11

95 Which of the sons of Sebastian Bach introduced a new system of fingering in clavichord playing?

96 Give an account of the earlier years of Handel.

97 What was Handel's first opera? His first oratorio?

98 From what earlier work was the *Acis and Galatea* of Handel in part derived?

99 When and where was Handel's *Esther* first performed?

100 Who was the most favoured rival of Handel?

101 Where was the *Messiah* first performed, and with what result?

102 Give a list of Handel's Oratorios.

103 A German contemporary of Handel was much admired by the Italians, who named him "the divine Saxon." Give his name.

104 Who was the composer of *Der Tod Jesu?*

105 "Mozart was greatly impressed with the beauty of *Medea.*" Who composed the opera referred to?

106 In what respects did Alessandro Scarlatti improve the opera?

107 Name some of the principal masters of fugue in the eighteenth century.

108 When and by whom was the Italian Opera introduced into France?

109 Who is regarded as the originator of the overture?

110 Give an account of *Les Bouffons.* What influence did they exercise upon the lyric stage in France?

111 State the circumstances of the rivalry between Gluck and Piccini.

112 Who is generally regarded as the founder of the modern symphony?

113 Name the principal operas of Mozart.

114 Who added to the accompaniments in the *Messiah?*

115 What was the *Liedertafel?* Who organized it?

116 Which of the French composers in Beethoven's time was in his opinion "the most estimable of living musicians?"

117 How many symphonies did Beethoven write?

118 What was the original title of the opera *Fidelio ?* State what you know of the history of this work.

119 To what cause did Beethoven owe much of his command of orchestral resources?

120 What was the nature of Beethoven's physical affliction, and at what period of his career did it become apparent?

121 In what capacity was Hummel considered a formidable rival of Beethoven?

122 Name the most remarkable of the operas composed by Spontini.

123 Relate the circumstances attending the death of Weber.

124 It is said that Weber introduced a new feature in the treatment of the opera-overture; what was it?.

125 Who composed *The Erl-King ?*

126 When and under what circumstances was the *Lobgesang* produced?

127 Who was the founder and first director of the Leipsic Conservatorium of Music?`

128 On what occasion was the *Elijah* produced?

129 What is a remarkable characteristic of Chopin's music?

130 Name a celebrated motett by Dr. Crotch.

131 Give the name of the composer of a concert-overture, entitled *The Wood Nymph.*

SECTION II.

132 Write out, from memory, the principal musical epochs and events of the first five centuries after Christ.

133 Who was the principal musician of the eleventh century?

134 What remarkable musical event took place in Germany about the year 1200?

135 About what period did Franco introduce the system of mensurable music?

136 Name the principal musicians of the fourteenth century.

137 In the fifteenth century, three celebrated composers were born the same year. Who were they?

138 What was the prevalent "School" or style of the thirteenth century?

139 Name the principal contemporaries of Tallis, i. English; ii. German; iii. Italian; and assign to each his characteristic as a composer.

140 Give the date of the introduction of copper-plate engraving for the printing of music.

141 Two celebrated English composers died the same year in the sixteenth century. Name them.

142 At what date was the Violin introduced into England; and by whom?

143 Give the date of the production of the first opera.

144 Give the title and date of the first Oratorio.

145 When was the harpsichord introduced into England?

146 Give the dates of the first German, English, and French Operas respectively, with their titles and authors.

147 When was the *Macbeth Music* published?

148 In one year of the seventeenth century two great German musicians were born. Give their names.

149 Who were Purcell's contemporaries at home and abroad?

150 Give the dates of the production of Handel's *Esther, Messiah, Israel in Egypt.*

151 When was introduced a new system of fingering for the clavichord, and what was the principal innovation?

152 In what year took place the first Handel commemoration?

153 When was the bassoon introduced into the orchestra?

154 When was Haydn's *Creation* produced?

155 Name the principal contemporaries of Beethoven.

156 In the year 1809 a great German master died, and another distinguished German composer was born. Name them.

157 Give the dates of birth and death of Beethoven.

158 Give the dates respectively of the invention of pedals to the harp and of the double action by Érard.

159 Name six of the most distinguished French composers of the present century.

160 Give a list of the leading English musicians during the reign of Queen Victoria.

SECTION III.

161 What were the Ambrosian chants?

162 Describe the antiphonal mode of singing.

163 Define the terms *Decani, Cantoris, Precentor.*

164 Can you account for the origin of the modern major and minor scales?

165 Write out the following " Gregorian modes," marking the semitones: Dorian; Phrygian; Hypo-Lydian; Mixo-Lydian.

166 Give specimens of *Organum* or Diaphony, as practised by Hucbald or Guido.

167 Write out the divisions of the great stave of eleven lines.

168 Of how many lines did the stave generally used in the thirteenth century consist?

169 Who is supposed to have founded a Chair of Music at Oxford?

170 To whom is attributed the invention of the Canon ?

171 Define *Counterpoint, Canon, Cantus firmus.*

172 Who is to be regarded as the first composer of modern music ; and for what reason ?

173 What was the art of Descant ? Faburden ? Write a specimen of the latter.

174 Describe the orchestra employed at the performance of *L'Anima e Corpo* by the direction of the composer.

175 Give a list of the principal composers of Oratorio.

176 Enumerate the movements in the *Missa Sollennis* of the Roman Church.

177 What distinguishes the Requiem from the ordinary Mass ?

178 Name any composers who have written Requiem Masses.

179 Describe the various kinds of Anthems in use in the English Church.

180 Can you name any peculiarity in the construction of the " Old Hundredth ? "

181 Describe the Madrigal, and give a list of the most noted composers of madrigals.

182 What is *basso continuo ?* For what purpose was it introduced, and what is the principal use made of it in the present day ?

183 Name four operas which may be regarded as so many landmarks in operatic history.

184 What are the principal theories of Richard Wagner in regard to the musical drama ?

185 Who was Metastasio ?

186 What English monarch employed a band of hautboys ?

187 Describe some of the principal dance forms in the *suites-des-pièces.*

188 Mention some of the most distinguished writers of *suites.*

189 What is a " Sonata ? "

190 Name three great composers who assisted in establishing the modern binary form.

191 Define the term *Musica di Camera.*

192 What is the place of the Concerto in instrumental music?

193 Name any well-known composer who has written a Concerto for the Flute?—for the Clarinet?— for the Organ?

194 Define the Symphony, in the old and in the modern sense.

195 Who is the "father of the modern Symphony?"

196. Give instances of the employment of the harp in oratorios by Handel.

197 Describe the Spinet, the Virginals, and the Harpsichord.

198 Mention some of the earliest makers of the *hammer-clavier.* What is the name usually given to this instrument? and for what reason?

199 Describe the more important varieties of the Lute.

200 Give a brief account of the ancient viol family, and describe the principal bowed instruments now in use.

201 Describe the old Cornet, Recorder, and Pilgrim's Staff.

202 How do you account for the higher compass of the trumpet as indicated in the orchestral scores of the last century?

203 Name as many as you can of the principal organ-builders of the eighteenth century, mentioning the improvements introduced by some of them.

204 Mention some of the most celebrated amongst English Organists.

205 What great French composer made a special study of the effects to be obtained from the drum?

206 Mention some of the greatest female singers of the last and present centuries.

LIST OF MUSICAL EXAMPLES.

LIST OF MUSICAL WORKS

MENTIONED IN THE TEXT.

GENERAL INDEX.

Festa, i. 27, iii. 22
Fétis, iii. 50
Field, i. 64, iii. 29
Fingering, i. 40
Flageolet, iii. 42
Flauto traverso, iii. 42
Flotow, i. 66, iii. 25
Flute, i. 4, 5, 32, 33, iii. 16, 27, 31, 32, 42
Flute-à-bec, iii. 42
Folksongs, i. 17, iii. 22
Forkel, iii. 50
Form, iii. 29, 32
Franc, Guillaume, iii. 21
Franchinus, iii. 50
Franco of Cologne, i. 16, iii. 7, 50
French Opera, i. 44, 49, iii. 24
Frescobaldi, i. 34, iii. 27, 29, 46
Froberger, iii. 46
Fugue, i. 20, 34, 44, 48, 51, iii. 18, 28, 50
Full Anthems, iii. 20
Fux, i. 47, iii. 18, 50

Gabrieli, A., i. 30
Gabrieli, Francesca, iii. 48
Gabrieli, G., i. 30, iii. 45
Gade, N. W., i. 68, iii. 32
Gaetano, iii. 39
Gaffurius, iii. 50
Gallia, Maria, iii. 48
Galliard, iii. 27
Gallus, i. 35
Galop, i. 60
Galuppi, i. 43
Garrett, iii. 20
Gauthier, iii. 39
Gavotte, iii. 27
Geminiani, iii. 41
German opera, iii. 24, 26
Giardini, iii. 41
Gibbons, Orlando, i. 36, iii. 20.
Gigue, iii. 27   [22, 46
Glee, iii. 23
Glockenspiel, iii. 47
Gloria in Excelsis, iii. 18
Gluck, i. 45, 46, iii. 25, 26, 43
Gluckists and Piccinists, i. 46, iii. 26
Goddard, Arabella, iii. 38
Goss, J., i. 65, iii. 20, 23, 50
Gossec, i. 44, iii. 32

Goudimel, i. 21, 29, 35, iii. 21
Goudok (Russian fiddle), iii. 40
Gounod, Ch., i. 66, iii. 25
Graun, i. 42, iii. 17, 18, 25
Graziani, iii. 29
Greek scales, i. 2, iii. 1
Green, iii. 46
Greene, i. 38, iii. 20
Gregorian chants and melodies, i. 13, 24, 29, iii. 2, 4, 21
Gregorian modes, i. 10, iii. 2
Gregory the Great, i. 10—14, iii. 6, 48
Gresham College, i. 26
Grétry, i. 44, iii. 25, 30—32, 50
Grisi, iii. 48
Guarneri, iii. 41
Guglielmi, i. 43
Guido, i. 15, iii. 5—7, 50
Guilmant, i. 66
Guitar, i. 3, 33, iii. 16, 39

Hackbret, iii. 39
Hale, Adam de la, i. 17, iii. 10
Halevy, i. 61, iii. 25
Hallé, Charles, iii. 38
Hammer-clavier, iii. 38
Hampel, iii. 45
Handel, i. 41, 42, iii. 17, 20, 24—27, 29, 31, 35, 39, 42, 43, 46, 47
Händl (Gallus), i. 35
Handlo, de, iii. 50
Harmonics, iii. 50
Harmony, i. 4, 14, 16, 17, 19, 26, 32, 38, 44, 49, 65, iii. 4, 30, 48,
Harp, i. 3, 4, iii. 35   [50
Harpsichord, i. 32, 33, 37, 40, 41, 47, 48, iii. 16, 17, 22, 27, 29, 31, 37, 38
Harpsicon, iii. 37
Harris, iii. 46   [46
Hasse, i. 42, iii. 18, 25, 26, 31, 32,
Hassler, Hans Leo, i. 35
Hatton, J. L., i. 65
Hauptmann, i. 57, iii. 30
Hautboy, iii. 27, 32, 43, 44
Hawkins, iii. 50
Haydn, i. 47, 49, 53, iii. 17, 18, 29—32, 40
Haydn, Michael, i. 49
Hebrew airs, i. 8
Helmholtz, iii. 51

www.ingramcontent.com/pod-product-compliance
Lightning Source LLC
Chambersburg PA
CBHW030837270326
41928CB00007B/1093